The MARRIAGE SECRET

by Bill and Christina Marshall

HAMMOND®
INCORPORATED

MAPLEWOOD, NEW JERSEY 07040

Library of Congress Cataloging in Publication Data

Marshall, Bill C.
    The marriage secret.

    1. Marriage.   I. Marshall, Christina Mae,
joint author.   II. Title.
HQ734.M422   306.8   80-16959
ISBN 0-8437-3349-7

PRINTED IN THE UNITED STATES OF AMERICA

FOREWORD

This is a delightful book. Bill and Christina Marshall have centered it around an aspect of marriage that has heretofore been too neglected. Their "secret" is an important idea, and they develop it in a creative and provocative way. The many situations they relate from their counseling experience illustrate the secret, and they gradually introduce the reader to ideas that all of us can use to achieve fulfulling relationships. Their refreshing use of humor and sensitive humanity make the book both pleasant and absorbing reading.

The Marriage Secret is original, timely, and engagingly on target. I recommend it enthusiastically to those married couples who need help in coping with the inevitable ups and downs that are inherent in all worthwhile human endeavors.

Wesley R. Burr, Ph.D.
Brigham Young University

CONTENTS

PREFACE

The Marriage Secret is different from other marriage manuals. Its main thrust is not to improve communication, although effective communication is unquestionably vital to a good marriage. Its major areas of concern are neither decision making nor problem solving, although these skills are absolutely necessary if married life is to progress smoothly. Neither is *The Marriage Secret* concerned specifically with openness or contracts. While these topics enter into *The Marriage Secret*, they are not central to it.

It is not our intention to rehash what has already been covered by other authors. Rather, we want to illuminate an aspect of marriage that we have never seen discussed in print, even though people struggle with it everyday.

The reader of *The Marriage Secret* may wonder why the first person singular is used throughout the book when the title page lists two authors. The answer is fairly simple. The book is written from Bill's point of view because he is the practicing marriage and family counselor. The case studies, experiences, and observations derived from his years of practice must be related, of course, from his vantage point. However, organizing this mass of raw data into a coherent and, hopefully, inspiring form requires the sensitive ear and practical experience of a trained writer. Hence, the collaboration. Together we have drawn from Bill's accumulated data an idea that can help you succeed in marriage if you incorporate it into the way you think and act. We hope you will do just that.

THE MARRIAGE SECRET

This book would not be complete without our acknowledging those who have contributed significantly to its concept and construction. At the most basic level, we acknowledge the work of Dr. Abraham Maslow, whose humanistic approach to psychology has greatly influenced our view of the world and man's place in it. We also wish to thank Dr. Wesley R. Burr for his assistance with the chapters on decision making and problem solving. Finally, we appreciate the efforts of our editor, Lonye Rasch, who helped us refine and clarify the marriage secret itself.

Bill and Christina Marshall

CHAPTER 1

The Marriage Secret

People in love are under the influence of the most violent, most insane, most elusive and most transient of passions and they are required to swear that they will remain in that excited, abnormal, exhausting condition until death do them part.
— George Bernard Shaw

Ralph, a young man of thirty-two, sat across from me, berating his wife, Susan. He complained that Susan was lazy and a poor housekeeper; that she never wanted to participate in the things he enjoyed, like camping and boating; that she nagged him constantly; and that she seemed unable to keep within any kind of budget.

This type of scene was not new to me. As a practicing marriage and family counselor, I spend several hours a day listening to husbands and wives chronicle each other's faults. Nonetheless, I was struck again by the irony of the situation. Here was a man describing to me the "terrible" person he lived with, seeming to forget that she was the woman he had asked to marry him! After all, he had chosen her and pursued her, courted her and spent time with her. Had none of the qualities he found so distasteful now been apparent then? Likewise, she had chosen him. Were none of the things she now found impossible to live with in evidence then?

Most of my clients insist that their partners have changed since they married them. It is my contention, however, that in many instances they have simply been revealed. The longer I counsel, the more convinced I become that *people do not really know each other when they marry*. This frightening but well-documented verity is the key to understanding what I call the "marriage secret."

I came upon the marriage secret as the result of a study I began in graduate school and continued throughout the first five years of my practice. Concerned by the rising divorce rate (one out of three) and by the percentage of married people who seriously consider divorce at some time in their marriage (seventy percent), I began to collect case studies of successful and unsuccessful marriages. I asked couples what had originally attracted them to each other and what, if anything, was now causing trouble between them. As courtship is the forerunner to marriage, I hypothesized that a major cause of divorce must be something inherent in our dating process.

Consider the Data

The following case studies are representative of the hundreds I have collected:

1. Pete and Lily grew up together in a small rural town. They were friends through grade school and dating partners through junior and senior high. They married two years after graduation because "it was the most natural thing to do." Both felt comfortable and secure entering into a relationship with someone they knew so well. After five years of marriage, they were divorced. Pete accused Lily of flirting outrageously with men at parties and in the neighborhood. He complained that Lily could not cook or keep an organized household, and that she showed no interest in improving her homemaking skills. Pete said he had always been a loner, but now Lily constantly nagged him to take her to parties or to invite company to their home.

Lily decried Pete's stick-in-the-mud attitude and insisted he had enjoyed company as much as she did before they were married. She claimed she had always been friendly and outgoing, and that only after marriage did Pete interpret her behavior as flirting. Lily said she had never been the domestic type, but Pete had always thought she would learn to be when she had her own home.

2. Ken and Doris met in a college English class and found they shared many interests. For hours at a time, they would happily dissect novels, plays, and movies, or discuss politics and philosophy. After graduation they married, and two

years later they were divorced. Ken and Doris indicated that they were attracted to each other because they could communicate so well. Why then a divorce? Because, they said, they just couldn't talk to one another! They argued over money, career plans, where to live, how many children to have, and so on.

3. Tom and Linda were "made for each other." At least that is what their high school yearbook said. Tom, captain of the football team, was voted "best-looking" by the senior class. Linda, a cheerleader, was elected homecoming queen. Soon after graduation they were married, but they were divorced six months later. The reason? They did not have anything in common. They were bored with each other.

As my file of case studies grew, I found that everyone faced at least one postnuptial revelation about his or her spouse's personality or habits. Usually there were many revelations. This was true whether the couple had known each other three days, three months, three years, or all their lives. It was true whether their backgrounds were similar or as different as night and day; it was true whether they shared the same interests or enjoyed few of the same activities. It was simply true that the married couples I interviewed did not know many significant things about each other.

It seems that our culture's romantic approach to courtship makes it extremely difficult to reach the real person we are dating. Why? Here are five reasons:

1. In attempting to be attractive, we hide *our* faults.

2. When we feel strongly attracted to another person, we disregard *their* faults. When we like half of someone's personality, it's easy to ignore the other half — at least until after marriage, when that personality becomes totally involved in our lives.

3. While dating, it is easy to mislabel character traits. For example, the person who is moody we might romantically call "mysterious," "reserved," or "sensitive." The spendthrift appears bright and charming. The jealous person is seen as protective. The person who thinks he is never wrong, we label "confident." However, after marriage, the confident, charming, protective, sensitive person we dated becomes the moody, jealous, know-it-all we are now married to.

4. By the same token, the issues that are important to a dating relationship are not the same ones that are crucial to marital success. For example, two bubbly, outgoing people who agree that disco dancing is fun, Christmas shopping terrific, and practical jokes a riot, may make a great dating couple, but not necessarily a great married couple. When people marry, they become involved with more practical matters such as how to budget money, whether or not to spank their children, whether to buy a car or a house.

The dating milieu is not conducive to conversations about unromantic topics such as money, power, housekeeping, or the nitty-gritty of child-rearing. Consequently, while a couple is dating, these topics rarely come under discussion. Yet, after the wedding, they must be discussed if the marriage is to have any chance of success. Whether or not to spank children is not an issue that must be resolved before two young people go out to a disco for a good time. However, when the first child arrives, its resolution is crucial to the unity and happiness of the marriage.

5. Sometimes dating partners do not ignore differences of opinion. They simply convince themselves that their sweethearts will change. For example, before marriage a woman may state categorically that she does not want children; that she intends, instead, to pursue a career. Still, her husband is secretly confident that she will, of course, change her mind

a few years down the road. Happily, he goes on daydreaming about his son, the "Little League star."

To recap:

> We hide ...
>
> We ignore ...
>
> We mislabel ...
>
> We don't agree on relevant matters ...
>
> and
>
> We believe our loved one will change after marriage.

The end result is that, in varying degrees, everyone marries a stranger. I have found that casual dating partners know as much about each other as do formally engaged couples.

Even living together for an extended period before marriage does not seem to overcome the five obstacles to knowing each other that I've just outlined. Marriage entails intricate legal, familial, and social obligations that cannot be duplicated on a trial basis. Columnist Sidney Harris once observed that "living together prepares a couple for marriage about as successfully as boot camp gets men ready for war." Boot camp and cohabitation both lack the same important element: the psychological aura of the "real thing." Living together is not being married; and for whatever complex reasons, people hold part of themselves back until they *are* married. An interesting story from a *McCall's* article by Susan Jacoby, entitled "Couples Who Live Together: The Surprises After Marriage,"* serves to illustrate this point:

> Julie and Bill Hawkins did not expect their lives to change when they were married in 1976. They had already been living together for three years, and they thought they knew everything there was to know about each other.
>
> They were wrong. Bill and Julie, both high-school teachers in a suburb of Detroit, are among the many

*June 1978

American couples who find that marriage *does* change their relationship — even though they began living under the same roof long before the wedding ceremony. Marriage can be better or worse than living together, but it is always different . . . .

"If we were sure of one thing, it was that we knew all of each other's quirky habits," Julie said with a smile and a slight blush. "All the time we were living together, we slept in the nude. The first winter we were married, Bill came to bed wearing a pair of flannel pajamas *I* had never seen. I asked him why, and he said he was always cold in the winter without pajamas but he hadn't wanted to admit it. The point is, there were certain things about our real selves that we didn't bring out into the open before we were married."

"My real self sleeps in pajamas from December till March," Bill said. "The strange thing is, I never even thought about it all the years we were together. I suppose I was trying to glamorize my image a little."

"I guess it's a kind of final letting go of fakery," Julie interrupted thoughtfully. "It's as if you've made the biggest promise you can to each other and you realize that, no matter how close you were before, you were still doing a little bit of pretending . . . ."

Quirky habits—like wearing flannel pajamas— are only the tip of the iceberg. The deeper level of commitment represented by marriage affects everything, from the way long-established couples handle their money to their relationships with relatives and friends.

Only in the area of sex has living together proven effective in "weeding out" couples who are not compatible. Obviously, couples who do not get along sexually rarely live together for an extended period, let alone marry. In other areas, such as money management, role definitions, and relationship to other family members, most couples report surprises and changes after marriage.

While it seems that living together before marriage ought to eliminate many potential areas of conflict, the research to date indicates otherwise. Professor David Olday, reporting in the *Cohabitation Research Newsletter, No.5* , found that couples who had lived together before marriage scored virtually the same on marital satisfaction and degree of conflict as couples who had married without previously cohabiting.

It is also interesting to note that couples who live together prior to marriage have, as a group, the same divorce rate as married couples who did not.

Of course, people who live in the same place must learn many things about each other; but, to some extent, they still play games. One researcher reported that practically every couple she interviewed used phrases like "letting go a little" and "bringing your real self out in the open" to describe their behavior after marriage.

For whatever reasons, people who live together still tend to hide, ignore, mislabel, fail to agree on relevant matters, and believe their loved one will change after marriage.

If, then, we all are unaware of what we are getting into when we say "I do," why are some marriages successful?

Why is Couple A, who knew each other only six months before they married, still together after twelve years, while Couple B, engaged for two years, is divorced after a brief marriage? Why does one couple, who share a common background, fail, while another couple, with very different backgrounds succeeds? Social scientists hypothesize that the more alike marriage partners are, the better chance they have for a successful marriage. The fact is , however, that no degree of similarity or careful planning can guarantee success.

As I again reviewed my case studies and considered the marital histories of clients and friends, I was struck by an odd idea. What if marital success were all a matter of luck? Luck, pure and simple. After all, people are so complex that *it is virtually impossible for one person to know all there is to know about another*. Therefore, people are lucky if they manage to marry someone who does not surprise them in irritating or even unbearable ways.

They are lucky too if an initially acceptable spouse does not change, in time, into someone less compatible, perhaps even intolerable. A close call with death, a religious experience, a new set of friends may change them. And there is little one can do to foresee, let alone prevent, changes that a spouse may undergo in the future.

It must also be remembered that even if your spouse does not change, your situation might. Accident, illness, and financial reversals are just a few of the things that can affect marriage in ways nobody anticipates. Some lucky couples never experience damaging intrusions into their marriage, while others are dealt a series of severe blows. Of course, one might argue that hard work and planning will keep things on an even keel. But this is only true up to a point. I know many couples who planned ahead and worked hard and then suffered tragic events, regardless. The luck of the draw? Why not? Nothing seems to explain it any better. Is luck, then, the deciding factor between success or failure in a marriage?

Many of my clients have felt they were victims of deceit. Things did not proceed as they had expected. They had vague feelings of anxiety and despair, and it was hard to pinpoint their origins. Now the origins of such feelings were clear: They arose from an awareness that one is *not* in complete control of the events that affect one's life. Certainly, if people could understand and accept the part that chance plays in their lives, they would be better prepared for the inevitable surprises in marriage.

I was sure that in the final analysis, luck determines what a couple has to deal with. But does luck also determine whether people deal *successfully* with what life brings them? If it did, I would be out of business. All the sound advice and helpful direction in the world could not overcome fickle fate if, in truth, fate always prevailed. Once more I read through a number of case studies. I remained convinced that the element of chance is indeed an important part of marriage, an aspect whose emotional impact had not yet been explored in depth. At the same time, there was an important truism that could not be ignored, a principle basic to my profession: *People can cope.* They can adapt. When it is their intention to make adjustments in their lives, they can change by design. Two couples can experience similar unexpected events; one will be torn apart by it, while the other copes and carries on.

The secret to successful marriage, I realized, could not be simply luck. Rather, it had to be how people handle, philosophically and in action, the part that luck plays in their lives. Everyone knows that luck determines the cards a poker player is dealt. Yet winning the game depends as much on the player's skill as it does on the cards. Likewise, in marriage, we must accept the hand we are dealt. Nevertheless, how skillfully we play our hand determines whether we win or lose.

The secret to successful marriage, then, can be condensed into the following proposition:

IN EVERY MARRIAGE, SUCCESS OR FAILURE DEPENDS ON HOW A COUPLE HANDLES WHAT LUCK HANDS OUT.

CHAPTER 2

Behind the Marriage Secret

Luck affects everything; let your hook always be cast; for in the stream where you least expect it, there will be a fish.

— Ovid

THE APPARENT EXCEPTION

Most people, even when they agree with the "marriage secret," are sure there must be exceptions. Often they think they know of one. Their "exceptional" couple usually profiles like this:

Karl and Wendy considered marriage very seriously. They knew they had strong feelings for each other and enjoyed being together. They also realized that marriage was more than a lifelong date. They knew that there were many important subjects that had to be discussed and agreed upon before they committed themselves to marriage. This they systematically did. With loving concern, they carefully explored each other's feelings on a variety of important topics and resolved differences where they found them. Happily, they anticipated enjoying a wonderful marriage. Now that they are married, everything seems to be going according to plan. They are a happy, well-matched couple.

Of course, this kind of preparation for marriage eliminates a lot of risk. Still, even here, luck plays a part.

Let me explain.

Recently, Paul and Sara, a couple with a history very similar to Karl and Wendy's, came to me for help. Like Karl and Wendy, they had taken preparation for marriage seriously. In earnest, they tried to uncover and resolve areas of disagreement before taking their vows. They felt they had done a thorough job. After two years of marriage, however, Sara was at her wit's end. Paul had a number of little habits that irritated her. He snored all night, and nothing seemed to help. When immersed in a book or a newspaper, he constantly sniffed and cleared his throat in a way that made her skin crawl. He left the toothpaste cap off, the toilet seat up, and his toenail clippings on the carpet. Sara felt silly and petty but could not keep her feelings from sending her into depression. Nothing she did could prevent her husband's habits from diminishing the awe in which she had once held him. There is no way to tell what will develop in a marriage.

Luckily, Karl did not have any irritating habits with which to surprise Wendy. But it was not their careful planning that prevented the appearance of petty problems, for they had not discussed snoring and toothpaste caps. Karl simply did not have the annoying habits.

Of course, Karl and Wendy's careful planning was unquestionably effective in reducing the number of surprises in their marriage. Certainly, it greatly lessened the chance that serious problems would arise. Still, no amount of planning can account for all the aspects of a human personality. Over the years, any married couple will discover new things about each other. If the couple is lucky, these will be good things; if not, effort will be required to work things out.

SO WHAT?

Once people accept the "marriage secret" as valid, the next question they ask is, "So what? It's all very interesting, but what practical application does it have?"

Of what use is it to realize that it is impossible to know all there is to know about another human being, and that you must be prepared to handle surprises in life and marriage?

All of you have made discoveries about each other since you said, "I do." For some of you, the discoveries have been unpleasant but easily dealt with. For others, the discoveries have been shattering. Some of you find yourselves wondering how you could ever have married your spouse. You wonder what happened to the person you fell in love with and how two people who used to have such a good time together could be at odds so often now. To you, the "marriage secret" says:

> Forget the person you *thought* you married
> and get to work on your relationship with the
> one you *did* marry.

Accept the fact that you did not really know each other when you married. The person you are married to is different from the person you courted. Unfortunately for both of you, the difference is not appealing. Nonetheless, continuing to moan or kick against the realities of these facts cannot help the marriage. Continuing to wish that things were like they were during courtship will not help. If you want your marriage to progress, rather than regress, you must begin where you are. Accept the idea that surprises, and adjustments to them are a natural part of living with an unknown quantity.

Of course, it is difficult to give up the notion of young love, no matter how old we are. We like the idea of living happily ever after, based solely on romantic attraction. This romanticism is the substance of our dreams. But dreams are not reality, and romance rarely provides an adequate basis for a lifelong relationship. Accepting the unexpected and adjusting to it does.

CHAPTER 3

Living with the Marriage Secret

Man must accept responsibility for himself and the fact that only by using his own powers can he give meaning to life.

— Erich Fromm

THE MARRIAGE SECRET

The marriage secret is not an easy proposition to accept. Those of you who believe that you cause things to happen probably find the instrumental role that luck plays a bitter pill to swallow. Yet all of you, at some level of consciousness, are uneasily aware of your own vulnerability. You sense there are things about your spouse you don't know, and you realize you cannot predict how his or her personality might change in the future. You understand that accident, illness, financial reversals or change in job, location, or religion could all intrude upon your relationship.

Many patients come to me suffering from depression because they feel completely at the mercy of circumstance. Their marriage is not what they had envisioned on their wedding day, nor is their relationship with their spouse what it had been in the past. Their dreams all seem doomed to die. Frightened and distrustful, they think their spouse has cheated them and that life is persecuting them.

How can such a barrage of negativism possibly be overcome? How should a person handle this "uneasy awareness" of Lady Luck's inconstancy?

I have found that there is a general attitude — a *weltanschauung*, if you will — that effectively prepares people to deal with surprises from their environment and their spouse. This point of view asks you to incorporate three major ideas into your way of thinking:

First:

Life is capricious; therefore, the unexpected is a natural part of existence.

Over the years, I have noticed that whether or not people are happy with what they have depends on what they expected to get. Two people living under similar conditions may experience very different feelings. All the research supports this observation.

If you expect your life to proceed exactly as you have planned, you will probably be disappointed. If, on the other hand, you expect that you will have to make adjustments along the way, you are much better prepared for the realities of life. I have known people to be devastated by an unforeseen turn of events, not because the events themselves were catastrophic, but because they were, in fact, unforeseen. These people have no knack for adjustment. They adhere strictly to the plans they have made. They acknowledge no route to happiness but the one they have mapped out beforehand.

Susan was such a person. She came from a small western town. Shy and retiring herself, she married a local boy who shared her temperament and plans. As the years went by, her husband began to excel in his job. He rose from workman to foreman to assistant manager. He was then offered a promotion to the main office, which meant a transfer to Salt Lake City.

The idea upset Susan a great deal. She had never thought she would have to make such a decision. What Susan expected even less was that her husband would seriously consider the offer; however, flattered by the proposal and intrigued by the role of executive, Susan's husband was definitely considering the move. At the same time, he was discovering some things about himself. He had changed from the shy, unambitious person Susan had married. Proficient at his job, he gained confidence. Recognition of his work stirred his ambition. He felt that he deserved to be promoted and he believed he could handle the job.

Susan was devastated. She reacted as though he had been transformed into a monster. In actuality, he was still very much the gentle, quiet man she had married. Only in this one aspect had he changed. Still, Susan felt betrayed.

She agreed to make the move because family and friends pressured her to do so, but she made no effort to adjust. She refused to recognize anything positive about her new surroundings. Her husband tried to work out compromises, but she would not support the plans. She wallowed in bitterness. This was not what she had expected from life, and she would destroy herself and her marriage before she would alter her plans. In therapy, she only reiterated her desire for things to be as they were before the job was offered. She would not accept the fact that wishing things were the same was not a solution. How poignantly apropos the title of Thomas Wolfe's *You Can't Go Home Again.*

Remember:

How you feel about a situation depends largely on what you expect. If you expect the unexpected, you will be prepared to roll with the punches. By anticipating the capriciousness of life, you will be better equipped to cope with negative turns.

This is not to say that a hedonistic philosophy is best. The person who believes he should eat, drink, and be merry for tomorrow he dies will never accomplish much. The people I know who handle life most successfully are those who plan and dream, then work to achieve the goals they have set. At the same time, these people understand that while their careful planning and hard work will increase their chances for success, nothing can guarantee it. They do not nail their lives to a rigidly explicit outline. They are reasonably flexible. In the wake of change, they use their energy to adjust. In the face of trouble, they focus on working out a solution or starting over again. Of course, they experience disappointment, frustration, and sadness. But their energy is not long wasted on these things. This flexibility finds its roots in their awareness of the unpredictable nature of life.

Second:

Life can do anything to you but determine your attitude toward what is happening. That prerogative is entirely your own.

It has been said many times that you cannot exercise absolute control over the events in your life. After marriage, your spouse may exhibit behavior or reveal beliefs you find upsetting. A variety of contingencies external to your marriage may intrude upon the relationship to change you, your spouse, or the situation in which you both find yourselves.

What you *can* control, however, is the attitude you take toward people and predicaments. That you have the ability to choose your attitude in any given situation is one of your greatest privileges, and therein lies also your greatest potential for making a success of your life. Nothing, and no one, can guarantee that you will have health, wealth, and uninterrupted happiness; but you can guarantee *yourself* that you will have patience, strength, and cheerfulness.

Even under the most wretched conditions this principle holds true. Viktor Frankl, a world-renowned psychotherapist who lived through the horrors of Auschwitz during World War II, found meaning in his suffering by arriving at a very similar conclusion. In his book *Man's Search for Meaning*[*] he writes:

> We who lived in concentration camps can remember the men who walked through the huts comforting others, giving away their last piece of bread. They may have been few in number, but they offer sufficient proof that everything can be taken from a man

[*]Published by Beacon Press, copyright 1959 by Viktor Frankl.

> but one thing: the last of the human freedoms – to
> choose one's attitude in any given set of circum-
> stances, to choose one's own way.

When one person maintains a constructive attitude, it often causes others to behave in a similar manner—but not always. I have patients who have learned to greet anger with calm, who strive to understand rather than condemn, who look for the interesting and humorous in life. After some initial confusion, their mates usually react by responding in kind.

Nonetheless, the bottom line is that people will do what they will do and events will happen as they will happen. These things cannot be determined by your attitude alone. Still, *you* determine what kind of person *you* will be as a result of life's ordeals, whether they be day-to-day problems or catastrophic events. A man who loses his leg may allow that misfortune to disfigure his relationship with family and friends as well, or he might face this personal tragedy courageously and get on with living. This is not to say that his grief and pain should never find expression. Grief is appropriate, but only for a while. If prolonged, it becomes destructive.

In college I had a remarkable friend. Her name was Cheryl, but everyone called her "Noodle." She was tall and athletic, cute but not stylish. A mutual acquaintance once quipped that if Florence Nightingale were crossed with a St. Bernard puppy, you'd have Noodle. I think he was right.

Noodle knew everyone—from the biggest man on campus to the shiest intellectual. She seemed totally unaware that distinct social groupings existed on campus. She considered everyone she met her friend and, as a result, was herself considered a friend by the most amazing assortment of people.

She had her quiet moments, her thoughtful times. And let me assure you that her life included its share of sadness. Like the rest of us, she was sometimes the target of other people's anger. She got her share of sarcastic remarks. Girls who resented her popularity made her the brunt of cruel pranks. Yet, in four years of association, I never heard Noodle say a mean or spiteful thing about another human being. She always gave the other person the benefit of the doubt. Like Anne Frank, she believed that people are good. She found life exciting; she approached her days with enthusiasm. When she suffered reversals, she would "pick herself up, dust herself off, and start all over again." Too good to be true? Almost. I have known very few people like her.

Henry David Thoreau once commented that "Man is the artificer of his own happiness." That statement could be expanded, for man is also the builder of his own sorrow. Your attitude lies before you like clay. What kind of person will you mold?

Third:

It is important to find fulfillment in the doing as well as in the achievement.

Married couples make many plans together. They plan careers; they start businesses. They set goals for themselves and for their children. We are an extremely goal-oriented society — an advantage, for it makes us "doers."

Objectives in life are important — no question. But so is proceeding toward them with love and humor. People who grasp the capricious nature of life understand that the things they struggle to achieve can be quickly taken from them. What also must be remembered is that what we experience while working toward our goals — the learning, the fun, the sharing — cannot be taken from us.

THE MARRIAGE SECRET

Driving to my office one morning, I noticed a man busily scraping chipped paint from a small building that had been empty for over a year. Every morning for the next three weeks, and sometimes in the evening as well, the man worked on the building. He cleaned and scraped and painted. He reworked and remodeled every aspect of the structure. Sometimes his wife helped him and they seemed to enjoy working together. It seemed a real, all-American, Mom-and-Pop venture.

Three weeks from the morning that work had begun on the building, the pair busily stocked their store with beanbag furniture of every color, size, and design. That evening as I passed, the man and his wife were hoisting a sign atop the bright little structure they had created. The sign read: NEW DESIGNS IN FURNITURE. In my rearview mirror I could see them hugging each other as they looked at the sign.

The next day, road-working crews moved in and ripped up the pavement for a half mile on both sides of New Designs in Furniture. A workman said that the city planned to widen the thoroughfare for several miles. For three months the roadwork dragged on. Heavy rains and an avalanche of difficulties delayed the project. I could just see the store before I had to turn and follow the detour around the work zone. Bright pennants cheerfully announced the "Grand Opening" of New Designs in Furniture. Every morning the man stood dejectedly in front of his business. Cars were allowed to worm their way through the clutter to reach stores along the torn-up street. Few bothered, however, to plod through the mess to reach even the established shops, and almost none made the effort to enter the new, unknown furniture shop. When finally the roadwork was done, New Designs in Furniture was gone. I assume the couple did not have sufficient cash reserves to last out the siege.

Scenes of the man and his wife working together on their project still float through my mind. I see them cleaning and painting, kibbitzing and laughing. I see them hugging each other after crowning their effort with a sign.

I often wonder how their marriage was affected by the episode. Did one of them blame the other for the store's failure? Were they discouraged to the point of despair, and, if so, did their despair make them bitter? Certainly they had a right to be disappointed. I only hope they understood the value of what they experienced together while working toward their goal, despite the fact that they did not reach it. Individual steps that move one closer to an end are important in their own right. Joy and satisfaction can be found in the journey toward as well as in the arrival.

After my wife and I had completed college, we hit upon an idea we knew could be built into an empire. One of the local church groups had sold hot, honeyed slices of home-made bread at an open-air camper show. The project had been a smashing success. We were sure the idea could be adapted to shopping centers and malls. What better treat than a thick slice of fresh, hot, homemade bread with honey-butter, jam, or melted cheese? We determined to give the enterprise a trial run at our county fair to work out any bugs before borrowing money to go big time. Today the county fair; tomorrow, the world!

Unfortunately, as it turned out, our booth was located as far from the entrance gates as possible. By the time people reached us, they were already stuffed with cotton candy and corn dogs. Many commented how good our bread looked and how they wished they'd known it was available. (They weren't the only ones who wished it!) Then electrical failure shut down our microwave and turned off our fridge. The bread was not hot; the milk went sour. The fair ran one week, and when it closed we had made over three hundred loaves of bread, spent many excruciating hours behind an unpatronized counter, and were out $250 for our efforts.

As we sat at home counting the receipts from our final night and figuring out just how badly we had done, there was no denying our feelings of depression. We had worked hard; we had suffered considerable embarrassment; and we had lost money. Quite a bit for us at that time. Yet, even as we sat there, we knew that we had shared an important experience. We had dreamed, planned, and worked together. In the process, we had grown together. There had been several hilarious occurrences during the week. We had both been charmed and fascinated by the "carny people" who made their living trailing their booths from fair to fair. We agreed that what we had enjoyed about the "great bread enterprise" and what we had learned about life and each other could not be dismissed by the flop of our venture!* True, the ending was unhappy, but the story had been full of new experiences and interesting people.

Whenever you set out to reach a goal, try to value and enjoy what you do as you work toward it. Never allow the immediate to be completely consumed by the future. What you hope for is important, but so is what you have.

In counseling, I try to help couples understand that many marital goals, such as better communication or more trust, should also be approached by emphasizing the means, not the end. That's obvious, you may say, but there are a great many people who are so goal-oriented that they set out to achieve a delicate goal in marriage like salesmen striving to increase their commission.

Married couples with problems often become extremely impatient with each other. This is especially true after they have had just enough counseling to agree upon what needs

---

*Malls across the country now sport bread shops exactly like the one we envisioned, which twists the knife a bit.

changing. Often, I find that people don't realize how hard their spouse is trying to change. They only know that their spouse is not changing as fast as they would like. It's a human foible to judge ourselves by how hard we try, while judging our spouses by how much they are changing. Progress is a more measurable and observable quantity.

If I can persuade couples to focus on the mate's effort to improve rather than the rapidity of the improvement, I find that their attitude changes. They become more patient and supportive. In this improved atmosphere, marital difficulties are more easily overcome.

Consider teaching a five-year-old child to add. The child can count into the hundreds and knows, to the count of 20 at least, what quantity each numeral represents. In other words, he or she knows basic arithmetic, but knowing how to count is not the same as knowing how to add. This is something the child must learn.

Sometimes the child becomes flustered and guesses at an answer. He hasn't reasoned it through, but, feeling pressure from you, he makes an attempt. If pressured too much, he may become immobilized and unable to reason at all. Wise and loving parents do not push their child through a learning experience. They know that as the child's knowledge expands, their relationship with him can grow only if they, the parents, are patient instructors. Few things can match the excitement and wonder of watching a child learn—with the possible exception of watching an adult learn.

As a child understands the basic elements of arithmetic, so a husband or wife may understand the basic elements of social interaction. This does not mean, however, that he or she knows how to behave as the other would like. For example, a person who comes from a family where affection is not expressed openly may have to *learn* how to express affection. If a husband fails to show affection for his wife openly, it may be because he *doesn't know how*. Would you call a child who had not been taught addition spiteful if, when asked to, he could not properly add two figures together? Yet, many of my patients believe their spouses are being spiteful if, when asked to, they do not become more openly affectionate. Remember: Many marital difficulties can be overcome only if one of the spouses undergoes a learning process. If your spouse is trying to learn a new kind of behavior, focus on his or her *attempt* to learn. Concentrate on the effort as well as the result you hope the effort will produce.

Impatience can be banished if a couple is enthusiastically involved in each other's *becoming* as well as their *being*. When the process is as interesting and valuable to a person as the goal, that person is far less likely to be impatient for the achievement of that goal.

People with this attitude see marriage as an ongoing process of patient discovery; a lifetime of getting to know each other, of teaching and learning. They have plans and they work hard, but they do not defer all gratification to some time in the distant future when their dreams suddenly come true. They enjoy the *now*, and they find all aspects of life and living interesting for what they are at the moment, not just for what they may contribute to some vague future objective.

Incorporating these ideas into your philosophy of life will help you to deal with life's capriciousness. Remember: Life can do anything to you but determine your attitude toward what is happening. That prerogative is entirely your own.

CHAPTER 4

Owning Your Feelings

*We are not the playthings of our passions;
it is we who choose them.*

> — Robert Goodwin Olson,
> *An Introduction to Existentialism*

Because your attitude is your one sure line of defense in an unpredictable world, it is important that the notion of a self-determined attitude becomes a real part of your life. One way to transfer this idea from the realm of thought into the realm of action is to own your feelings.

ACKNOWLEDGE YOUR RESPONSIBILITY

When you own your feelings, you verbally acknowledge that you are responsible for the way you respond to people and events; you are accountable for your feelings — positive and negative.

We are fond of such sentences as, "You make me so angry" or, "You make me so happy." What actually happens, however, is that another person acts a certain way and we respond to that with anger or happiness. Our feelings come from inside us. No one can *make* us feel anything.

What you feel is an expression of who and what you are: your background, your parents, your education, your experiences. In these, you are unique. Therefore, what bores you may delight another. What you find humorous, someone else might consider insulting. What terrifies you may seem merely interesting to the person next to you.

Burt, Helen, and Ralph

Let's look at a situation which illustrates that feelings are in response to, but not caused by, a given stimulus.

One evening Burt, Helen, and Ralph hear their neighbors, the Scrappers, having another knock-down, drag-out fight. Burt closes his window and thinks, "It makes me feel so sad to hear people talk to each other that way." Helen opens her window wider and thinks, "Boy, it makes me feel good to hear her give it to that bum!" Ralph hovers tentatively over his phone, wondering if he should call the police. "It makes me feel frightened to hear people fight like that," he thinks.

Three people are simultaneously exposed to the same situation. Each person responds differently.

The truth of the matter is that the Scrappers did not *make* anyone feel anything. They were the stimulus to which each person responded according to who he was and what was going on inside of him. What Burt meant is, "When I hear the Scrappers fight, I feel sad." Helen meant, "When I hear the Scrappers fight, I feel good that she is giving it to the bum." Ralph meant, "When I hear the Scrappers fight, I feel afraid for their safety."

A Significant Difference

You are probably saying, "Picky, picky, picky! What possible difference can it make if Ralph says, 'It makes me afraid to hear people fight like that' rather than, 'When I hear the Scrappers fight, I feel afraid.'" Granted, the difference in words is minimal. The difference in meaning, however, is most significant.

When you continually use sentences such as, "You make me so angry," you imply that your emotions are at the mercy of external forces. Even when you say, "You make me so happy," you imply that if you are not happy, it must be someone else's fault; he or she failed to make you happy.

With this attitude, you set yourself up to be victimized by people, situations, and happenings outside yourself. *You* do not decide your mood or your ability to function; *they* do. *They* make you angry, sad, or worried. You have no choice in the matter.

The only way to combat this "victim syndrome" is to view your emotions as independent of what is going on around you. Your feelings do not operate on the same cause-and-effect basis as a chemical reaction. If a chemist takes four samples of silver chloride solution and exposes them to sunlight, each will, without exception, turn into silver metal and chloride gas. There is no parallel for this kind of relationship in the world of emotions. If four people are exposed to a spider, for instance, all four may react very differently.

"There's a spider," one might say languidly pointing to the hapless arachnid.

"How interesting, a Phoneutria Nigriventer!" another might comment.

A third person might shriek, jumping from her chair to dust furiously at her pant legs.

A fourth person might leap aggressively across the room and, in a brisk display of courage, stomp the little critter into oblivion!

No one can control another person's emotions the way a scientist can control a chemical reaction. While silver chloride has no choice but to react in a particular way when exposed to sunlight, people can, to some degree, choose how they react to a situation, even though their feelings often seem to be automatic.

CHOOSING YOUR FEELINGS

Many people bridle when I say they can *choose* their feelings. "Don't feelings simply happen?" they ask. "Surely no one can decide what he will feel."

I realize that most feelings arise with the speed of an automatic reflex. Someone calls you a nasty name and you feel hurt. It's that quick. You hear a strange sound in the night and you feel fear. You do not consciously decide to feel fear, but for whatever reason, fear is the reaction you have to a strange sound in the night. Once an emotion emerges, however, your right to choose comes into play. You can decide to let the emotion continue or even grow, or you can try to change it into something else.

For example, a wife who discovered *why* her husband behaved in a way annoying to her learned, through counseling, how to move quickly from initial annoyance to sympathy. After a while, she reported that she no longer felt annoyed at all. Her initial response to the behavior now became sympathy. She had, in effect, conditioned herself to respond sympathetically. It is our unique set of experiences that constitutes who we are. By adding the experience of counseling, this woman was able to change her emotional response to her husband's behavior. Further, by exhibiting sympathy and understanding rather than annoyance, she supported her husband in his efforts to change and, with her help, he was able to alter his behavior.

Nothing in your environment can force you to feel something you do not allow yourself to feel. You decide how you will respond to any given stimulus. If a tactless spouse comments, "You really ought to join the spa; it could get you back in shape," a variety of alternatives are open to you. You could become angry that your spouse implied that you are out of shape. You could feel hurt. You could feel sad that someone you thought was your friend said that. You could feel embarrassed and allow the comment to lower your self-esteem. You could feel sorry for your spouse that he or she needed to build his or her ego at your expense. You could interpret the comment as a show of concern for your health and feel grateful. You could even feel it was funny that your overweight, underexercised spouse would dare to comment on your shape. The choice is yours.

What you cannot do is say, "Claude hurt my feelings, so now I'm depressed and acting very peevish. It's not my fault I'm acting this way; it's Claude's, because he hurt my feelings." When you understand that you chose to allow yourself to go along with your initial reaction to Claude, you will see that you are being peevish because you decided to be.

OWNING FEELINGS AND THE MARRIAGE RELATIONSHIP

Recognizing the concept of owning one's feelings can contribute in three major ways to a more positive marital relationship. First of all, owning your feelings can help you control your negative, destructive impulses. Second, it can help you be more specific about what upsets you. Third, it can reduce the amount of mutual blame that presently exists in your marriage.

1. *Controlling Negative, Destructive Impulses*

When we behave nobly or demonstrate patience, understanding, or kindness, we gladly take credit for the emotions we exhibit. When, on the other hand, we are short-tempered, fussy, or otherwise obnoxious, we prefer to pass the buck to someone or something outside ourselves. Owning our feelings, however, makes passing the buck much more difficult.

When you acknowledge ownership of your feelings, even if only to yourself, it is hard to be negative and destructive. Most people will reconsider their attitude if they hear themselves saying something like, "Things are really getting to me today, so I have decided to be cross" or, "When George made that comment about my hair I felt put down, so I have decided to be petulant all evening."

Sometimes I ask my clients to make an attempt at home to express their feelings to themselves and to each other in this manner. After a few weeks, they often report that being spiteful, sarcastic, or unkind in any way is not as easy as it used to be.

It is one thing to act negatively when the blame can be placed elsewhere. It is another thing to act negatively when you must shoulder the responsibility yourself. A professor, under whom I took a theology class in college, made a comment I have never forgotten. He said that if you are planning to do something you know to be morally wrong, do not allow yourself to rationalize about it. Say in a straightforward manner, "I am planning to do this thing. I know it is wrong, but I want to do it and I am going to do it." It's amazing how difficult it is to do something against your moral code when you approach the action from this standpoint. Owning one's feelings has something of the same effect. How much easier it is to feel irritable when you can rationalize that you are the victim of someone who has made you feel that way. Yet, most people are very uncomfortable admitting that they have chosen to be irritable.

I am reminded of a woman named Kathy who had a violent temper. She was easily set off, and her husband decided that he had taken all the verbal abuse he could endure. In counseling, she complained that her fits of anger were not her fault. Her husband made her so angry, she said, that she could not control herself. We discussed the concept of owning one's feelings, and she was finally persuaded that her angry explosions were in response to, but not caused by, her husband's behavior. I agreed that in some ways she had reason to be upset. Her husband's actions had, at times, been inappropriate. Nevertheless, she was still responsible for the ways in which she responded to his provocation. Although their problems were serious, I felt they could be worked through if, and only if, Kathy could learn to control her temper. If she would accept the idea that she *chose* to be angry, she would be able to see that she could also choose other, more constructive feelings.

Finally, she agreed to change the structure of her speech. She would no longer say or think, "He makes me angry."

Instead she would say, "When he does _____ , I decide to be angry." After several months of phrasing her emotional sentences in this way, Kathy found she was better able to control her outbursts. She said she found it very unpleasant to think of herself as deciding to indulge in one of her fits. It was more comforting to see herself as deciding to be patient or understanding. Of course, there were still times when she felt too angry to attempt to find a more constructive emotion. Then she would say, "When you _____ , I feel so angry." But because even this sentence indicated that being angry was her responsibility, she did not feel free to launch into a full-fledged attack.

Recognizing that her feelings were her own had been crucial to Kathy in learning to control her temper. Once she could refrain from her outbursts, the couple was able to involve themselves effectively in solving their problems. Eventually, they put their marriage on a more even keel.

2. *Being More Specific About What Upsets You*

Unfortunately, people and events sometimes provide adequate reasons to choose negative emotions. When you believe you are experiencing righteous anger, you may decide to go with that feeling. If you do, your partner should know that when he/she acts in a certain way, you feel angry. This is also true for feelings like hurt, embarrassment, or sadness. These emotions are not positive, but they are sometimes appropriate. They become negative only if they lead to depression, acts of retaliation, or decreased self-esteem. Your spouse should know not only *when* you are feeling these emotions, but also *what part* he/she plays in the situation.

A prevalent problem is that people often tell their spouses how they feel *before* they specify what they are responding to. Most people phrase emotional statements like invitations to a brawl: "You make me so angry!" "You hurt my feelings." "You really embarrassed me tonight." These statements are accusations. "You make me so angry!" can be a very general indictment. Does everything about your spouse make you angry? Or is it a particular thing your spouse said or did? In the face of a general indictment, the accused spouse goes on the defensive, and people on the defensive don't make very good listeners.

The person who owns his feelings excludes broad accusations from his emotional statements. He is more interested in specifying his response to a particular behavior. A person could easily begin a conversation with his spouse by saying, "You hurt my feelings." Accusatory statements stand on their own very nicely. But when you own your feelings, your statement asks to be prefaced with something. It sounds awkward to begin with, "I felt hurt." You are forced to be specific about what is bothering you: "When you dismissed my comment as uninformed, I felt hurt." Consider the difference between the following dialogues:

I

(Husband and wife arrive home from a party.)

HUSBAND: All right, what's the matter?

WIFE: What do you mean?

HUSBAND: You tell me. All I know is that you wouldn't talk to me all the way home.

WIFE: Okay, I'll tell you. You really hurt my feelings this evening. *(Wife accuses husband of hurting her feelings, but he doesn't yet know what she's referring to.)*

HUSBAND: What?

WIFE: And you embarrassed me too. *(Husband is attacked again.)*

HUSBAND: What are you talking about? I didn't do anything to hurt or embarrass you this evening. *(Husband is becom-*

ing defensive before he knows specifically what his wife is referring to.)

WIFE: You said my dress was too tight right in front of all those people. *(Husband now knows what his wife is referring to, but his defenses are already activated, making it harder for him to focus on what he did and his wife's feelings about it.)*

HUSBAND: Oh come on, don't be so sensitive. I was joking. Can't you take a joke anymore?

WIFE: That wasn't funny.

HUSBAND: Not to you, maybe. *I* thought it was.

WIFE: You think it's funny to hurt and embarrass me?

The couple is beginning to get off the subject of her feelings about his actions. The husband could easily shift the focus to his wife being a bad sport; or the wife, goaded by her husband's response, might accuse him of being cruel and malicious when all she originally felt was that he was insensitive.

II

(Husband and wife arrive home from a party.)

HUSBAND: All right, what's the matter?

WIFE: What do you mean?

HUSBAND: *You* tell *me*. All I know is that you wouldn't talk to me all the way home.

WIFE: Okay, I'll tell you. Tonight when you said in front of all those people that my dress was too tight, I felt hurt. I felt embarrassed too. *(Rather than hurling a general accusation, the wife specifies what she is responding to before detailing her feelings.)*

HUSBAND: I'm sorry. I didn't mean to hurt your feelings or embarrass you. I was just joking.

WIFE: I didn't think it was funny.

HUSBAND: I won't do it again, okay?

WIFE: Okay.

It would be unrealistic to claim that owning your feelings will make such an exchange calm and friendly. These exchanges are always tense. Still, owning feelings can help prevent the conversation from becoming an ugly argument. In the second dialogue, the exchange is less abrasive. The wife does not accuse her husband of hurting or embarrassing her. Instead, by owning her feelings she is able to state exactly what she is talking about (her husband's comment) *before* explaining how she feels (hurt and embarrassed).

It always amazes me that some couples can argue on and on when neither one is certain what they are talking about. So many arguments begin when one spouse or the other starts off with a "You make me _____" type of statement. Defense mechanisms swing into action before the discussion is ever focused on a particular behavior. Sometimes, in the heat of the ensuing argument, that focus is never clarified. In contrast, when the spouse acknowledges responsibility for his/her own feelings, it is almost always clear what he/she is responding to.

3. *Avoiding the Blaming Syndrome*

Blaming each other is chronic in many troubled marriages. When couples come to me for counseling, our first session often reveals two people who have zeroed in on each other's faults. Each one believes it is the other's shortcomings that have caused the marriage to founder. Each one has come to counseling confident that I will "fix" the partner. Believing the focus of our sessions will naturally be on their spouse, many people are surprised when attention is given to *their* behavior.

This blaming syndrome feeds on the "You make me _____" type of statement. When a husband says to his wife, "You make me sick, flouncing around, flirting with everyone at every party," that statement hands the wife the whole ball of wax. *She* flounces. *She* flirts. *She* makes him sick. Everything is *her* fault. Many an insecure man married to a naturally outgoing woman experiences extreme, though totally uncalled for, jealousy. In actuality, the true cause of the jealousy is within them. They should be looking at themselves, not their wives. Owning their feelings would be a solid step in the right direction. If the husband says, "When I see you flouncing around the room and flirting at parties, I feel jealous," he is forced to share the spotlight with his wife. She is responsible for her actions, but he is responsible for his feelings. If, in addition to owning his feelings, the husband agrees to give a photographic description of his wife's activities, his part in the problem becomes even clearer. He says, for example, "When I see you talking with other men in a friendly way at a party, I feel jealous." Obviously, the problem is as much his as hers.

Rarely is one spouse solely responsible for the problems in a marriage. Marital difficulties are almost always created jointly. The responsibility may be split fifty-fifty or twenty-eighty, but it is split!

Acknowledging that you have a problem is the first step toward solving it. Owning your feelings is one way for you and your spouse to stop blaming each other. Look to yourself first, and you'll probably realize that while your spouse may have provided the stimulus, the response came from you.

FIGHTING THE VICTIM SYNDROME

As a child, you believed adults were in control of the world. What they said, went. What they wanted, they got. As you have grown into an adult, however, you probably have been disappointed to discover that it is only little children that you can command with much success. In all other areas, you must work, compromise, and keep your fingers crossed. Even after diligent effort, a gust from the winds of fate can blow your achievements away.

People do not always turn out to be what you thought. Events do not always proceed as you planned. It is often easy, even tempting, to see yourself as a victim of circumstance. The victim syndrome, however, must be combated if you are to emerge successfully from life's inherent crises. Owning your feelings will help you to fight the victim syndrome. You may not be able to control your circumstances. Your mate may surprise you with behavior you could never have imagined. Nevertheless, when you own your feelings you are reminding yourself that those feelings are yours, and yours alone. No contingencies of fate or mate can dictate those feelings. To accept responsibility for them is a giant step toward becoming a healthy person, independent and secure.

You cannot expect another human being to be accountable for your joy or sorrow. Others may be responsible for the things that happen to you, but ultimately, you decide how you will be affected by them. If you continue to use the "You make me _____" type of statement, you will continue to reinforce the idea that you are not responsible for what you feel. By actually changing the pattern of your speech and thought, you can continually remind yourself that you *are* responsible for your feelings. The more often you own your feelings, the more a self-determined attitude becomes an integral part of your life.

CHAPTER 5

Anger

*Whenever you are angry, be assured
that it is not only a present evil, but that
you have increased a habit.*

— Epictetus

The first real fight my wife and I had was over politics. Although she majored in political science at college, we had never seriously discussed political matters during our courtship. It was something of a shock to discover, six months into the marriage, that our political views on several issues were considerably different. What we fought over is not important. What is important is that what started as a discussion became an argument.

I could not believe she held the views she did. She obviously felt the same about me. Before we knew it, our frustrations had turned to anger, and our anger had turned our discussion into a fight. It is not in either of our backgrounds or personalities to yell when angry. Instead, the angrier we get, the quieter we both become. Eventually, we both stopped talking altogether. For the rest of the evening we did not speak to each other. For the first time in our marriage, we went to bed without even saying goodnight. I felt numb. We had promised each other that our marriage would be different; that we would always be able to talk to each other and exchange ideas without fear of ridicule or retaliation. What had happened? In all truthfulness, I had not expected this kind of behavior from either of us.

What had happened was that the incident marked the first time we had encountered an issue about which we strongly disagreed. We were both uncomfortable in the discovery of something we had not known about each other. (What else didn't we know?) Consequently, we both desperately wanted the other to convert to our way of thinking in order to put things back into equilibrium. If we could have discussed the issue, we might have resolved it in a way we both felt good about. However, our anger made an intelligent discussion impossible. As a result, we had an argument that ended by our not speaking to each other.

ANGER AND THE ELEMENT OF SURPRISE

I believe that almost all marriage problems come as something of a surprise. Few people marry expecting trouble. It is naturally a shock when they yell at each other or suffer through a period of sullen silence. People do not enter marriage expecting to be embarrassed by their spouses or bitterly disappointed in them. They do not expect to find themselves unable to talk to the person they love. Incompatibility and infidelity are not things people expect when they marry. If they did, they wouldn't get married. Even the fact that people argue before marriage does not seem to lessen the shock of marital fights. Somehow, it was all supposed to be different. Even when a trouble spot is well worn by years of confrontation, I find that people are still incredulous when this happens in their marriage. They were going to live happily ever after.

When you are unpleasantly surprised in marriage, you feel shocked, frustrated, hurt, sometimes afraid. The trouble is that most people move quickly from these initial feelings (hurt, fear, confusion) to anger. A friend of mine, who had led a rather sheltered life, married the man of her dreams and moved far away from her protective family. She assumed that all the aspects of her life that had once been handled by her parents would now be handled with equal skill by her new husband. Almost immediately, the couple fell into financial straits. Slowly, the girl began to realize that her husband was no better prepared to handle household finances than she was. Surprise! She was terrified. What would become of them? This fear she distorted into anger, and whenever they discussed financial matters she flew into a rage. The pattern continued for several years until finally, through counseling, the wife was able to identify the fear behind her fury and tell her husband about it. Their relationship improved greatly as she learned to express her fear rather than allowing it to become anger. The husband, in return, became less defensive as he realized that, in financial matters, he was not dealing with an acid-tongued shrew, but something closer to a frightened child.

People often respond with anger to the surprises in their marriage. They become upset when they are forced to recognize that their ideal vision and their real marriage are not congruent. They strike out at their spouse in an attempt to force him/her to be the person they thought they married. As you are probably aware, when someone is angry with you, you become defensive and, as the best defense is a good offense, you become angry in return.

Anger is a powerful emotion and particularly destructive, since it almost always precipitates ill-considered action: breaking a vase; yelling; refusing to speak. In the nine years that I have been counseling married couples I have often seen anger injure people and destroy relationships. I have come to the conclusion that anger does not contribute anything positive to life. Married couples — especially because they are committed to functioning as a unit — must learn other ways of responding to the unexpected. If you wish to achieve maximum success in your marriage, you must learn to restrict the intrusion of anger into your relationship.

VENTING ANGER

Is there a way you could eliminate anger from your life? Could you actually decide to remove a feeling from your repertoire of reactions? Surely, you may say, all you would be doing is suppressing a distasteful emotion, which is a neurotic and unhealthy practice.

However, I am not proposing that people suppress their anger; I'm suggesting that they learn to control it. It may not be possible for most people to eliminate feelings of anger totally, but they can most certainly learn to reduce the frequency and intensity of those feelings.

Most of the books I read while studying to be a marriage therapist made the point that feelings are neither good nor bad; they simply are. You cannot help what you feel, the books proclaimed; *you can control only what you do as a result of your feelings.*

This idea has been taken a few steps further and popularized into several forms of "Let it all hang out" therapy. People are taught that to suppress negative emotions is unhealthy; that to vent negative feelings enhances mental health. If you are angry, the theory goes, you should show your anger. Yell, swear, kick the door — do whatever enables you to vent your emotions (short of assault or major property damage, of course).

As it turns out, however, such indulgent experiences are not health-enhancing. Not a single study has shown that "letting it all hang out" has improved individual mental health or interpersonal relationships. In fact, studies have shown just the opposite to be true: Subjects who violently vented all their negative emotions suffered marked increases in tension and irritability.

CONTROLLING ANGER

Over the past several years, I have been helping my patients to understand more fully how their emotions operate. This understanding has, in turn, helped them respond to upsetting situations with feelings other than anger.

What I teach them is *the distinction between primary and secondary feelings.*

Primary feelings are those you show in reaction to a situation *first* — hurt, fear, frustration and insecurity, for example. Secondary feelings are your reactions to your primary feelings — anger, jealousy, and depression, for example. Feelings motivate actions. You are hurt, so you cry; you are happy, so you smile. Your ability to discover and deal with your motivating emotions is often the key to understanding and controlling your actions. Primary feelings can trigger secondary feelings. Insecurity can cause jealousy. Feelings of inadequacy can lead to depression. Your frustrations can build to the point that you become angry. Here again, dealing with the more basic, motivating emotions can help you understand and control the secondary emotions that are triggered by them.

FEELINGS

Primary	*Secondary*
hurt	anger
fear	depression
insecurity	jealousy
frustration	

Imagine that your child has run into the street in front of an oncoming car. The car stops in time and a tragedy is averted. You reach the child, angrily grab his arm, and shake him. You shout, "Don't you ever run into the street like that again!" As you grab the child, you are angry, but anger was not your first emotion. Your first emotion, as you watched your child run into the street, was fear. You passed from fear to anger very quickly, but fear was still your primary feeling. The anger was a distortion of your fear — a reaction to it — and, as such, a secondary emotion.

Understanding that these two categories of feelings exist will help ensure that your search for motivating feelings does not come to a stop at the more obvious secondary level. You must always attempt to get to the most basic feeling involved. Centering a discussion on primary emotions usually helps to reduce fighting and speeds resolution of a conflict.

John and his wife Susan had come to counseling complaining of a myriad of small irritations that had resulted in general unhappiness for both of them. They seemed to be constantly at each other and almost always angry. Like many couples, they could not specifically trace the genesis of their misery. It had developed slowly — incident after incident, angry reaction after angry reaction. They were stymied at the level of secondary feelings.

Susan's tardiness was one of John and Susan's many problems. John did not remember Susan being so undependable while they were dating, but, after about a year of marriage, it seemed she was late for everything. If she went out, she rarely came back when she said she would. If she was supposed to call for John at work, she was inevitably at least ten minutes late. John realized he was very tired of it.

At first, John complained and Susan promised to improve. But she didn't. By the time they had been married three years, John was reacting with increasing anger when Susan was late. Susan, who usually thought she had a good reason for being late, began to feel increasingly misunderstood and put upon. They described to me the following scene:

Susan went out in the evening to do some shopping. She said she would be home around eight o'clock. At nine o'clock she returned home. She had not called to say she would be late.

JOHN: *(his voice loud and angry)* Where have you been?
SUSAN: At the Mall. I'm sorry I'm late. I didn't know there was a sale on tonight. I got so involved, I lost track of time.
JOHN: You said you'd be home at eight o'clock, and it's nine. Why didn't you at least call?
SUSAN: I told you. I lost track of time.

THE MARRIAGE SECRET

JOHN: Well, if you're going to act so irresponsibly, maybe this will just have to be the last time you go out in the evening alone.

SUSAN: Now wait a minute, John, you can't ground me like some teenager.

And the fight is on . . .

Susan knows she has done a thoughtless and irresponsible thing, but now she is on the defensive and not likely to admit it. When John becomes angry with Susan, he causes her finely tuned defense mechanisms to swing into action. At that point, she is no longer willing or even able to discuss, consider, apologize, or change. She is ready only to defend or counterattack.

You may be saying that John has a right to be angry over such irresponsible behavior, but that argument is neither here nor there. John's anger, righteous or not, has obviously not caused Susan to change her behavior. His main objective is not to punish Susan, but to help her become more punctual because he does not like being married to a person who is always late. It is not something he expected when he married her.

After several sessions of counseling, John and Susan understood the difference between primary and secondary feelings and were beginning to recognize the more basic emotions that prompted their anger.

John came to realize that his primary reaction to Susan's tardiness was hurt. When she came home late, he felt she couldn't care less about him. When she was more than a half hour late, he worried that something had happened to her. John was able to pinpoint fear and hurt as the primary emotions that culminated in anger. I encouraged John to tell Susan how he felt. When he did, she was visibly moved. She had not thought about her behavior in terms of hurting John's feelings. It had not occurred to her that by being late she led John to feel that she didn't care about him.

I asked John and Susan to reenact the scene they had first described to me — only this time John would try to express his primary feelings rather than his secondary anger.

JOHN: *(with a calmer voice)* Susan, where have you been? I've really been worried.

SUSAN: I'm sorry I'm late. I didn't know there was a sale on at the Mall tonight. I got so involved, I lost track of time.

JOHN: I was afraid something had happened to you. I almost called the police to check the accident report. You know I don't mind your going out in the evening sometimes, but please call if you're going to be late. When you forget, I feel hurt that my peace of mind isn't very important to you.

SUSAN: *(sincerely)* I'm sorry. It was thoughtless. I'll try extra hard next time to remember to call if I'm going to be late.

Because Susan was in the habit of being late, she did not find it easy to change her ways. Nevertheless, she said she felt much more determined to adjust her behavior, now that she understood what effect it had on John. Susan had not particularly minded triggering John's anger — especially when she felt he was being picky or unjust. Nevertheless, she was not callous to hurting his feelings. That was something she did not want to be responsible for. John's plea for peace of mind had been much more effective than his threatening remarks.

When you become angry, you waste energy either quarreling or sulking — energy that would be better spent identifying and discussing your primary feelings. When John and Susan focused on the fact that John's feelings were hurt, they not only moved toward a solution to their problem, they also improved their overall relationship.

FOCUSING ON PRIMARY FEELINGS

Consider the sentences in the following columns. How would you respond if your spouse used the sentences on the left? Would you be affected differently if, instead, you heard those on the right?

How could you forget our anniversary!	I really feel hurt that you forgot our anniversary.
You might as well take your clothes and a sleeping bag to the office. You practically live there anyway!	I feel left out and unimportant when you spend so much time on your job.
Will you please stop using every fifty-cent word and technical term you know and just speak plain English for a change. Stop showing off!	When you use technical terms that I don't understand, I feel confused and inadequate. I also feel you're trying hard to impress me. Actually, I feel excluded from the conversation.

The sentences on the left are typical of what you might say when you are angry. They challenge your spouse to fight. They immediately put him/her on the defensive. The sentences on the right express your primary feelings. They are much more likely to initiate constructive conversation. Whenever you act or plan to act in a way that can cause conflict between you and your spouse, search yourself for the emotions that are motivating you, and then focus on them. Get down to the primary level. Make an attempt to express your primary feelings rather than the anger they have prompted.

Expressing primary feelings is much harder for some people than it is for others. For the person who is not emotionally oriented, talking about emotions is difficult. Some of you may find the idea of admitting you are hurt, afraid, or insecure very threatening. For you, exposing primary feelings may be like exposing a raw wound. Opening up emotionally makes you feel vulnerable, and perhaps you fear vulnerability. Even if you accept the idea in principle and understand how expressing primary feelings can enhance your marriage, you may find that the words just won't come out. Inwardly, you find it too dangerous to express your primary emotions.

But expressing primary feelings is a skill, and (as with any other social skills) while some people may have more natural aptitude, others can master it if they try. Start out with easier topics. Try the technique when emotions are not running high. Tell your spouse how someone other than he/she triggered within you feelings of hurt, fear, insecurity — possibly when you were a child. Choose a situation that is removed from you and your spouse by time and distance. Let me assure you, expressing primary feelings is a skill well worth learning. By the same token, if your spouse is insecure about expressing primary feelings, it is important to receive any such attempt with respect.

When you learn to focus on primary feelings and keep your attention there, you'll find that you have no need to suppress anger, *because you won't feel anger*. You may feel frustration, but not anger. Since secondary emotions camouflage primary feelings, dispensing with secondary emotions and focusing on primary ones is a way of getting to the heart of the matter, a way to open yourself up more fully. This is not suppression at all, but ultimate exploration.

Many of my clients have learned to stop the progression of their feelings at the primary level. When their spouse does something inconsiderate, they feel only hurt or disappointment. If their spouse doesn't understand something they are trying to explain, they feel frustration. When they see their spouse with an attractive person of the opposite sex, they feel insecure or inadequate. These feelings of hurt, frustration, or insecurity, however, do not become distorted into anger or jealousy, because these people deal with the situation at the level of their primary feelings. They have no need to suppress anger, because they do not move to that secondary level of feeling.

Impossible? Well, nobody is perfect, and even my clients have relapses. Still, those who are serious about improving their marriages quickly rein in their secondary emotions when they feel them surfacing. If something happens and they begin to feel angry, they try hard to find the primary emotion causing the anger and focus their thoughts and conversation on that.

A NAMBY-PAMBY APPROACH

Some of the people I counsel claim that if they don't get angry with their spouse, they never get them to change in any way. They believe that it is fear of chastisement that keeps their spouse "in line." One client, whose wife was frequently late for appointments, responded negatively when I tried to teach him to identify his primary emotions and work from there. "Sorry, Bill," he said. "I have a right to be angry with Grace when she is late. She deserves to catch it. If I took this namby-pamby primary-feeling approach she wouldn't have any reason to change her behavior, because she wouldn't have to worry about getting into trouble."

If fear of punishment or the desire to avoid ugly scenes were the only motivation for change in marriage, then this logic would hold true; but I have found, without exception, that if there is any mutual fondness in the relationship at all, angry confrontations are not necessary to initiate change. I know from the experiences of my clients that if you want to promote a change in behavior, it is far more effective to say, "It hurts my feelings when you're late and don't call; I feel you don't care that I'm sitting here worrying," than it is to say, "You are so inconsiderate; why didn't you call when you realized you were going to be late?" When you care about another person and learn that something you are doing frightens, frustrates, or hurts him/her, that knowledge is incentive enough to make you try to adjust your behavior. Conversely, if your spouse comes to realize how his behavior hurts you, he/she will also try to change. Of course, angry, sarcastic, or threatening remarks can force another person to do what you want. But think of the price your marriage pays.

JUST PLAIN MAD!

When I first introduce the concept of primary feelings to my clients, they often want to hang on to the idea that they are *just plain mad*!

"How did you feel when your wife hid the checkbook from you?" I asked one husband.

"I felt angry," he responded.

"What else?" I coaxed.

"Nothing else," he insisted. "Just plain mad."

If there is a kind of anger that is not preceded by a primary-level feeling, I have not encountered it. In every case of anger my patients have described, *the anger was a secondary feeling, a reaction to something that came before.* Shock, horror, disgust, fear, hurt, pain — something came before.

What I have encountered on a few occasions is anger so justifiable that the preceding emotions lose their importance. Reading about German atrocities during World War II or viewing films of Auschwitz, for example, can stir feelings of anger so overwhelming that their origins are of no consequence. The anger is, in a sense, righteous. Nevertheless, let me add a word of caution: *Righteous anger is rare.*

For the most part, insisting that you are "just plain mad" is a cop-out. It is easier to be angry than to reveal and discuss your primary feelings. Yet, I have never come across a situation where expressing anger was more beneficial to a marriage than talking about the primary feelings that motivated it.

As I discussed in Chapter Four, your attitude is your responsibility. If someone is cruel to you, you can respond with anger. Or you can respond with compassion, realizing that perhaps that person suffered some unfortunate experiences in life that caused him to become a cruel person. It takes more energy to be compassionate under stress than it does to be angry. The benefits, however, justify the effort. I have seen many couples learn to relate in increasingly positive ways as they tried to deal with problems at the level of primary feeling.

I've found that women seem better able than men to understand the importance of distinguishing between primary and secondary feelings. What they find hard to believe is that anger should not be expressed. "Shouldn't my husband know how I feel?" they ask. Unequivocally, yes! Marriage partners should know how their spouses feel. But remember: *Anger only covers up what you really feel.* It is a smokescreen that clouds rather than clarifies an issue. It is a distortion of your true, primary feelings.

ANGER AS A WEAPON

Anger can also be used as a weapon. If you wish to use it to punish, intimidate, or coerce in some areas of your life, that is your decision. You may believe that anger has its place when you deal with the mechanic who has failed to fix your car properly *again*, the snippy clerk who ignores you to chat with a friend, or the stranger who has just backed into your front fender. But in a marriage, coercion, intimidation, and punishment serve no good purpose. If the meal is not quite up to snuff, if the telephone conversation interferes with your TV viewing, even if your spouse is responsible for your crumpled fender, your reaction should not be one of anger.

OTHER ALTERNATIVES

When you are first learning to focus on primary emotions, you will probably find that you still give way to anger occasionally. At this point, there are several alternatives open to you that are preferable to acting out your negative emotions.

Many therapists, for example, would encourage you to verbalize your anger:

> "When you compare me to your mother, I feel angry."

The assumption behind this technique is that people who care for each other will respect each other's feelings. A wife who owns her feelings lets her partner know how she feels without putting him on the defensive. The couple should then be able to discuss the anger calmly and, hopefully, arrive at a solution to the problem.

I have found in my counseling, however, that any expression of anger can trigger defensiveness. When you own your anger, you definitely soften the defensive response in your spouse, but you rarely do away with it entirely. If you must express your anger, I recommend that you try the following two steps:

Acknowledge very specifically that the problem is yours:

> "When you compare me to your mother, *I can't handle it*. I feel angry."

Then ask for assistance:

"I don't want to be angry with you. I don't like the feeling. Please help me with this."

When one spouse is humble enough to ask for help, the other will usually respond to the plea. The stage is then effectively set for solving the problem.

If you find yourself losing control, excuse yourself from the situation. Signal your spouse that you need time to compose yourself. Say, for example, "I'm really too angry to talk about this now." Then set a definite time for continuing the discussion: "Could we talk about this after dinner?"

It is very important to establish a time for resuming the discussion so that the problem is not left to fester. The cooling-off period should not extend beyond twenty-four hours. Use this time to think about what caused your anger. Identify your primary feeling and return to the discussion ready to talk about what is *really* bothering you.

Remember, however, that these techniques are still secondary alternatives. If you can move directly to expressing your primary emotions, you will have a better chance of resolving your problems constructively. If you can say, for example, "When you compare me to your mother, I feel hurt and unappreciated," you (a) let your spouse know your feelings in a way that is least likely to put him or her on the defensive, (b) get directly to the point of what is bothering you, and (c) are well on your way to solving your problem. In other words, you contribute to the depth and scope of your marriage relationship.

CHAPTER 6

Using Your Five Senses: Checking Out

*The man who is afraid of asking is
afraid of learning.*

— Danish Proverb

THE MARRIAGE SECRET

It is a truism that things are not always what they seem.

What sounds like a baby crying in the night turns out to be the neighbor's cat.

A person who appears to be cold and haughty is really shy and insecure.

The laughter you think is aimed at your new hair-style is actually prompted by a slightly off-color elephant joke.

The things we see, hear, smell, taste, and touch are not always what we think they are. In marriage this can spell trouble.

When one spouse misinterprets the actions or words of the other, offense is sometimes taken where none was intended. My folders of case studies are overflowing with tales about husbands and wives who have been upset over something for a day, a week, a month, or longer, and who later learned it was not at all what they thought.

One wife was shocked and deeply wounded when her husband took off his wedding ring during an argument and laid it on the table. To him, the gesture was simply a way of emphasizing his point. To her, since the ring represented their sacred marriage vows, to take it off was tantamount to renouncing those vows.

A young husband of one year was horrified when his wife excitedly showed him the bedroom furniture she had picked out for their new home. The set included twin beds! He was so hurt and embarrassed he could not bring himself to challenge her selection. Obviously, he concluded, the honeymoon was over. She didn't want to sleep with him anymore and this was her way of telling him. What he didn't know was that her parents had always had twin beds. To her this particular bedroom set represented entry into the adult world. Her choice had nothing to do with sex.

A man who had been married for thirty years read a magazine article that inspired him to become more helpful around the house. In the evening, he would go through the house picking up things and straightening this and that. Occasionally he vacuumed or dusted. His wife thanked him every evening for his assistance and he felt good about his efforts. In reality, however, the wife was not happy. She interpreted his sudden interest in housework to mean that he thought her housekeeping skills were inadequate.

Misunderstandings of this kind are particularly unfortunate, for there are too many legitimate points of conflict in most marriages to waste time and energy on imaginary troubles. When you are surprised or upset by something your spouse does, take the time to find out if it was meant in the way you are taking it. Your energy should be spent on resolving areas of actual discord, not wasted on imagined offenses.

YOUR FIVE SENSES

To ensure that you direct your efforts toward real grievances rather than imagined offenses, you must first learn to differentiate the two. The place to begin is with your five senses. Consciously concentrate on what your senses are reporting to you. What you see, hear, touch, smell, and taste have an immediate impact on what you feel inside.

If you are uncomfortably hot, you become irritable.

If a person smells bad, you respond negatively to him/her.

If you go to an expensive restaurant and the food is not good, you are disappointed and become sullen.

Evaluate situations in terms of your senses. Remember, the way you interpret sensory input forms the basis for your feelings and your actions. What you sense is the beginning of what you feel and do. For example:

> Martha, a gourmet cook, *sees* John picking at the *coq au vin* she made for dinner. He pushes the food around and stares glumly at his plate. Martha interprets this to mean that John doesn't like the food. Because Martha worked hard preparing it, her feelings are hurt.
>
> As Martha thinks about how hard she worked, her hurt begins to turn to anger. "He could at least say *something*," she thinks to herself. For the rest of the evening, she is cross. When John finally works up the courage to ask Martha why she is upset, she snaps at him: "Nobody ever appreciates me."

John and Martha have a go at a few rounds of bickering as to whether or not Martha is appreciated. Finally, Martha confesses that her feelings were hurt because John didn't like the dinner. John protests that he thought the dinner was delicious, and the next fifteen minutes are consumed by a "I did — You did not — I did — You did not" argument.

Eventually, Martha gets back to what she *saw*, the scene that triggered the whole reaction:

> "But you just *picked* at dinner," Martha accuses.
> "I'm sorry, dear," John explains. "It really was delicious, but today at the office we learned that

our company is being bought by a large midwest conglomerate and we're all going to be fired. I was thinking, 'What is the best way to tell you to buy more hamburger than prime rib?' And I lost my appetite completely."

While it was sad that John was about to lose his job, even sadder was the fact that they spent the whole evening arguing when they could have been supporting each other in a time of crisis. If Martha had been in touch with her senses, she would have mentally traced the roots of her anger back to them as soon as she felt the anger starting to rise. Her thoughts would have progressed like this:

I'm angry. *Why?*
Because my feelings are hurt. *Why?*
Because I *see* John not eating the dinner I worked so hard to make.

The most basic element here is what Martha saw. That was the starting point for the whole episode. If we can force ourselves back to the sensory input that starts the chain reaction, we can get to the reality of the situation much sooner.

CHECK IT OUT

Once you have pinpointed what it is that's upsetting you, ask your spouse for an explanation. This is sometimes called "checking out." There are two basic ways to do this:

You can make a statement describing what you have seen, heard, etc., and ask your spouse for an explanation.

or

You can make a statement detailing your interpretation of an event and ask your spouse whether or not your conclusions are correct.

For example, the husband who was surprised to find his wife ordering twin beds could have said,

"I like the style of furniture, honey, but this set has twin beds. What does that mean?"

Or, using the second method of checking out, he might have said,

"The fact that you've picked a bedroom set with twin beds means to me that you aren't happy with our sex life. Is that right?"

In either case, the point of checking out is not to interrogate or accuse. Therefore, it is important to avoid an accusatory tone of voice. Checking out is a way of gathering information; a method of finding out what your spouse meant by his or her words and actions; a means of uncovering misunderstandings before they cause needless pain and estrangement in a relationship.

Let's replay John and Martha's scene, only this time with Martha aware of her senses and putting that awareness to use.

Martha begins to experience feelings of hurt, which then turn to anger. She traces them to their point of origin: seeing John picking at his dinner. "It could be that John doesn't like his dinner," she reasons, "but wouldn't it be better to check this out with John before beginning a wild spiral of interpretations that may be incorrect?" She decides to tell John what she is seeing and ask him to explain.

"You're not eating. Don't you like the dinner?" she asks. John uses this opportunity to tell Martha why he is not hungry.

Soon, Martha isn't hungry either. They find solace together.

Of course, it is possible that John simply didn't like the squab. Regardless, Martha's question would still have been beneficial to the relationship. John could still reply that although he doesn't like the dinner, he knows Martha worked hard and appreciates that. Martha may still be a little hurt, but she knows he appreciates her efforts, and a little appreciation can go a long way toward salving hurt feelings.

No matter what John answers, it is good that Martha asked.

It should be kept in mind, however, that checking out presupposes a certain amount of trust in a relationship. When one spouse checks out something he has seen or heard, he must have faith in the explanation his spouse gives him. If your spouse challenges an explanation you give, or if you have reservations about something your spouse tells you, then these reservations need to be talked through before the checking out can continue. Chapters Seven, Eight, and Nine will provide you with several ideas and skills to help you work through such problems. If, however, a couple finds that they constantly challenge each other's explanations, this is an indication of a much more serious problem in the marriage. A relationship void of trust is a relationship in need of professional help.

Nonetheless, where relationships of mutual trust do exist, checking out is a valuable tool — especially in uncovering the misinterpretation of an innocent act.

Just recently, a client of mine related an appropriate example. He and his wife had just finished making a difficult decision. As he left the room, a breeze from an open window across the hall blew the door shut with a bang. The husband did not give the bang a second thought. After all, he knew the wind had blown the door shut. His wife, however, assumed that her husband had intentionally slammed the door and decided he was upset over the compromise they had just worked out. Unfortunately, she did not follow after him to ask if he had slammed the door on purpose. Instead, she stewed over the situation all day long.

"Why did he agree if he didn't like the decision?" she wondered.

"Can't we discuss things like adults?" she fretted.

"What a childish thing to do!" she fumed.

By the time her husband arrived home that evening, his wife was angry and upset, and he didn't have the slightest idea why. An uncomfortable evening was endured by both of them until the wife finally spelled out what was bothering her and the husband explained the misunderstanding.

With rare exceptions, it is better to proceed from a position of knowledge than from one of ignorance. Reality rather than supposition should be the catalyst for our feelings. Too many people waste their lives suffering from imaginary slights.

Begin, then, by getting in touch with your senses. Be acutely aware of what you see, hear, smell, touch, and taste. If sensory input from your spouse disturbs you, check it out.

Unfortunately, there *are* husbands and wives who *intentionally* hurt each other. For revenge, perhaps. But usually people do not deliberately set out to hurt or upset others, least of all husbands and wives. In counseling I often encounter people who are thoughtless or insensitive, but I have rarely come across a person who is intentionally mean. Check it out! See what explanation your spouse has for what your senses report. Get information, get perspective, and as the Book of Proverbs counsels, "In all thy getting, get understanding."

Do not waste precious time and energy on imaginary problems. Save that for the real ones.

CHAPTER 7

Communication

The genius of communication is the ability to be both totally honest and totally kind at the same time.

— John Powell

Author of *The Secret of Staying in Love* and *Why Am I Afraid to Tell You Who I Am?*

There are many things people do not know about each other when they marry.

No matter how much they do know about each other, people continually change as a result of their experiences. The person you marry today will not be exactly the same person years hence.

Life is capricious. There is no way to exercise complete control over the events that intrude upon a marriage relationship.

These are the three truisms that so heavily affect a marriage. My main aim is to help you deal with them successfully. Although this book is not primarily concerned with communication, decision-making, or problem-solving skills, these skills do warrant our attention, since becoming adept at them significantly improves a couple's ability to handle the unexpected in life. Consequently, this chapter and the two that follow will introduce those communication skills, decision-making procedures, and problem-solving techniques that will help you deal more effectively with the element of chance in your marriage.

When two unique personalities try to mesh in the context of an unpredictable world, not all the parts of their puzzle will fit together immediately or permanently. Marriage is a lifetime of getting to know each other, of teaching and learning. A variety of subjects will need discussing; decisions will have to be made; problems will have to be solved as the couple gradually pieces together the picture of their lives.

COMMUNICATION VS. SENDING MESSAGES

Students of human interaction are fond of saying, "You cannot *not* communicate."

I take exception to that statement. It is perfectly possible for people to not communicate. We do it every day. What we cannot do is fail to *send messages*. Whether you are discussing the weather, making love, or sitting motionless in meditation, you are sending messages, verbal and nonverbal, which the people around you receive with varying degrees of awareness. Talking, shouting, crying, hitting, laughing, smiling, scowling, clenching fists, are all means by which we send messages. Nevertheless, just because messages are *sent*, or *received*, does not necessarily mean that communication has taken place. Sending and receiving messages are ways of exchanging information, but they are not communication.

When people are communicating, they are making a sincere effort to send and receive *correct* information. They are consciously striving to understand and be understood. Communication is not just talking. COMMUNICATION IS THE PROCESS OF TRYING TO UNDERSTAND EACH OTHER.

SET IT UP

When it is crucial that you and your spouse understand what you are saying to each other, some effort should be made to establish an appropriate climate for conversation.

This may be accomplished by briefly checking to make sure it is a suitable time to discuss a particular subject. For example, "Can we talk about the budget now?"

When your spouse says or does something that confuses or upsets you, signal him that you need to talk about it for a minute:

"Wait a minute. I don't understand that. Let's talk about it."

Sometimes setting up requires more formality and effort.

If, for example, you feel that a subject you want to discuss is sensitive or complicated, arrange a time when you can communicate uninterrupted — when the kids are in bed, or after your spouse's favorite TV show is over. Few things are more detrimental to effective communication than trying to discuss a subject when there isn't enough time to cover the issue, or when the situation is inappropriate to the topic. A backyard barbecue with friends, for instance, is not the place to discuss your sex life, if honest communication on the subject is your aim.

Communication can also be hindered if you jump into a discussion without telling your spouse specifically what you want to talk about. The traditionally oriented husband who does not like the idea of *his* wife working, for example, should not begin by complaining about the state of the housekeeping, laundry, meals, family correspondence, etc. Rather, he should open the discussion by saying that he is having trouble accepting the idea of her working and would like to talk about it.

If you feel it is important that your spouse hear you out completely on a subject before he/she responds, say:

> "There's something I want to discuss with you, but
> I want you to hear me out before you say anything."

"Setting up" gives your efforts to understand each
other a head start.

SET IT UP

Choose an appropriate setting.

Arrange for enough time.

Tell your spouse what you want to talk about.

Be specific.

Prepare your spouse not to interrupt you if there is something you want to get out before he responds.

ROLE REVERSAL

Many of the things that have already been covered in previous chapters will help you in your efforts to communicate. Maintaining an attitude of concern for your relationship and each other, flexibility, owning your feelings, discussing your primary rather than your secondary emotions, and checking out — all of these techniques will facilitate your attempts to understand each other.

There is, however, one additional aid that should be added to the list: *role reversal*. It is useful when one of two situations exists:

> You have *sent* a message and want to be certain that the receiver understood what you intended to say.

> You have *received* a message and want to be certain that you understood what the sender intended to say.

Role reversal can be time-consuming; it does not fit as easily into ordinary conversation as do expressing your feelings or checking out. When you or your partner decides that a role reversal is needed, you must purposely interrupt the conversation and say that you would like to reverse roles:

"Could we do a role reversal on this?"

The phrases used during role reversal are not subtle either. They openly signal that you want to make an effort to communicate at that moment. The standard phrases fall into two categories, differentiated by whether you sent or received information.

When you have *sent* a message and want to be sure that the receiver has understood it, you may ask,

What do you hear me saying?
How are you reading me?
Can you tell me what I just said?

When you have *received* a message and want to make sure you have understood it correctly, you might say,

I'm hearing . . .
I hear you saying . . .
Okay. I think I understand. Let me
see if I can explain it back to you.

Role Reversal: A Technique for Trouble Spots

Role reversal is not meant to be used extensively. It is a troubleshooter. It helps couples over trouble spots. If you find yourself in a situation where the harder you try to explain something, the more confusing and hostile the atmosphere becomes, do a role reversal. Then at least you will know if there is something to be hostile about.

If you feel you must discuss a topic that will trigger strong feelings in your spouse and you want to be sure that you are at least understood before your mate takes up the cudgels, request a role reversal. It can sometimes stop the argument you thought was inevitable.

Karl, a client of mine, was amazed to find that role reversal had helped him calmly discuss a very touchy problem with his wife, Becky, who is usually quite volatile. Karl had decided to try role reversal because he was concerned that Becky would be upset by what he had to tell her if she did not fully understand what he was saying. Their conversation went something like this:

KARL: Becky, I have something important to discuss with you. I wonder if we could do a role reversal on it to make sure we're communicating.

BECKY: Okay.

KARL: I know we've been planning to go to your family reunion next weekend at the lake, but there's been some real trouble at the store and I'm beginning to worry about being away for the whole weekend. I might be able to get things squared away, but if I can't, I just don't see how I can be gone both days. We could lose some important business. I know you've been looking forward to this and you should go even if I have to stay home. What I really want you to know is that I do want to go. I know I've said some things before about your family reunions, but since I've gone to a few I've gotten to know the people, and I was looking forward to this one. What do you hear me saying?

BECKY: I hear you saying that there are some problems at the store and you're not sure you can go to the family reunion. You would like to go, but you may not be able to work it out. You want me to go, whether you do or not.

KARL: That's about it, but I guess I didn't emphasize one thing enough, because you didn't pick up on it. I really *want* to go. I'm afraid that because of comments I've made in the past about your family reunions, you'll think that my need to be at the store is just an excuse not to go. I don't want you to be angry or hurt. It's important to me that you believe I was looking forward to the weekend. I'm not just trying to get out of it. How are you reading me now?

BECKY: Okay, I think I understand. Let me see if I can explain it back. You really want to go to the reunion. You are worried that I'll think you're trying to get out of it because of things you said before. You're worried that I'll be angry or hurt, so it's important to you that I believe this is not just an alibi.

KARL: That's right. . . . Do you believe me?

BECKY: Well, I'll be disappointed if you can't come, but I believe you. I'm not angry or hurt.

Karl had good reason to be concerned about what he was going to tell Becky. Obviously, he had made some disparaging remarks about her family gatherings in the past.

He rightly concluded that unless he could get Becky to understand the situation and how he was feeling, there would be trouble.

What do you think would have happened if Karl had simply said: "Listen Becky, about your family reunion, I want to go, but there's been some trouble at the store this week and I just don't think I can make it. You go, though, even if I can't."

Knowing Becky, I think she would have hit the roof. I also think that in the ensuing argument Karl would never have gotten Becky to understand his feelings. By asking for a role reversal *first*, Karl helped to ensure that Becky would at least hear him out before pasting him to the wall.

Role Reversal Works

Role reversal is not an easy communication skill to initiate in marriage. It is awkward and uncomfortable. You feel silly saying, "Could we do a role reversal?" "I hear you saying . . . ," or, "How are you reading me?"

Nevertheless, it is a useful tool because it works. Despite the fact that it seems staged and unnatural, role reversal is invaluable when it is important to you that a message you sent be understood, or when you need to make sure you understand a message that you received.

Once you realize that role reversal can prevent arguments from escalating and, in some cases, stop them even before they start, the technique no longer seems so clumsy. Also, couples who are willing to try it find that eventually they develop their own phrases to initiate and use during a role reversal. I can assure you that my clients who have made the effort to use role reversal at appropriate times have found it extremely helpful.

WHAT COMMUNICATION CAN
AND CANNOT DO

Communication is currently in the spotlight. Courses on improving communication are being taught all across the country. The theories sound good; the results look positive. Obviously, improving communication in a marriage must be a good thing. But wait! Nothing is obvious to a scientist. One group of social scientists decided it was time for a clinical test. Would you like the good news first or the bad?

The good news is that after improving their communication skills, forty percent of the spouses studied improved their marriage relationship.

The neutral news is that forty percent of the marriages were unaffected by improved communication. (It is possible that the couples did not use properly or consistently what they had learned, or that they may have already *been* communicating effectively before the study was made.)

The bad news, however, is a real shock. For twenty percent of the couples involved in the study, improved communication actually contributed to the deterioration of their marriages! In the marriages represented by this depressing statistic, improved communication served only to underline just how far apart the spouses were; how very different their basic values. Their problems and incompatibilities were accented. These couples needed to learn decision-making and problem-solving skills in addition to improving their ability to communicate.

Regrettably, many courses on communication skip these important areas altogether or, at best, treat them lightly. Most counselors and educators put the spotlight on communication. They believe it is the number-one problem in American marriages today.

I disagree. I would even go so far as to say that communication skills can actually be destructive if taught without equal instruction in decision making and problem solving. I understand the importance of communication. But communication should be viewed as a means, not an end; a tool to get a job done, not the job itself.

Of course, in some situations communication — understanding — is sufficient to resolve a conflict. If, for example, you learn that something you are doing is hurting the husband or wife you love, understanding that fact may be enough to make you change your behavior. But quick, easy resolutions occur only if the person being asked to change a behavior has no strong attachment to it.

For example: After a friend of mine and his wife had been married for about a year, she told him she was tired of his finishing her sentences for her whenever she paused to find just the right word. She said his actions made her angry. The word "angry" made him defensive, but his defensiveness dissolved as he came to understand through communication that anger was her surface emotion and that, on the primary level, her feelings were hurt. She considered his action an indication to her and everyone listening that he held her I.Q. in low esteem.

The husband was horrified to discover how embarrassed and hurt his wife had been by his actions. To him, finishing her sentences had been a natural extension of the team spirit that pervaded every other aspect of their lives. In his mind, since he and his wife thought and felt the same so often, finishing her sentence in the excitement of a stimulating conversation was like finishing one of his own. Now that he understood her feelings, however, he was anxious to change his behavior.

Understanding was enough because the husband had no stake in resisting. He really lost nothing by changing. But what if, in some way, finishing her sentences had been important to him? Would knowing he was hurting her feelings have been enough to make him change his behavior?

Several years ago, a couple came to me for counseling whose relationship suffered from a similar sore spot. In this case the husband was a college graduate and the wife was not. The man attached great importance to his educational status. He was easily embarrassed by his wife's unerudite comments at parties and family gatherings. He considered himself a gentleman and a scholar; his wife, something of a blockhead. Finishing her sentences or taking over conversations altogether was his way of protecting himself from embarrassment.

When the husband came to understand how much this action hurt his wife's feelings, this understanding was *not* enough to evoke change. He was not callous to his wife's feelings, but an appearance of academic acumen was extremely important to him. He had a genuine stake in making sure she did not embarrass him publicly.

At the same time, while the wife had come to understand her husband's obsession with the academic life and could see that finishing her sentences and taking over conversations was an extension of that obsession, she was not willing to let the matter pass. Her ego was also involved; her self-esteem was on the line. They had come as far as understanding would take them. Now they had a decision to make and a problem to solve.

CHAPTER 8

Decision Making

The color of truth is gray.

— André Gide

Every day we must make decisions. Most of them are of small consequence. Some have important but limited effect. A few influence the entire course of our lives.

Most married couples can handle the many small decisions that fill an average day, without resorting to any formal decision-making process. (I have encountered couples, however, who couldn't agree on what kind of juice to have for breakfast.) At the same time, when dealing with weightier matters, most couples could profit by improving their decision-making skills.

DECISION MAKING AND THE ELEMENT OF CHANCE

The element of chance is inherent in every decision. No matter how carefully you come to a decision, there is no way to determine how effective it will be until it is implemented. Unforeseen contingencies interfere. The desired results do not always follow. As in all human endeavors, factors beyond your control intervene.

Frustration may lead you to conclude, "Why bother to improve my decision-making skills? What's the point of plodding through an organized decision-making process if the outcome can never be assured? If life is unpredictable, wouldn't eeny-meeny-miney-mo be equally useful?"

But the truth of the matter is that improving your decision-making skills will increase the possibility that you'll make an effective decision, even though *there is no guarantee that all will go as you expect.*

In addition, by acknowledging the chance factor, you and your spouse are more likely to avoid blaming each other if something does go wrong. When you make a decision in your marriage, acknowledge to each other that although you have both done what you can to make this an effective decision, it may not yield the desired outcome. If it turns out later that there was a factor you both failed to recognize or could not have foreseen, and things work out poorly, don't blame each other. Always keep in mind that every decision has within it an element of chance. It's the nature of things.

My friends Allen and Patti had gone about buying their first new car ever so carefully. They had considered all the pertinent information they could gather on the makes and models in their price range. Finally, they agreed on a Chevrolet model, which had been named "Car of the Year" by several prestigious car magazines. Judging by the information they had collected, the car seemed the best choice. Unfortunately, their purchase was a mistake. For two years they had nothing but trouble. Speaking from the safe perch of hindsight, relatives and friends asked Allen and Patti why they had bought the car in the first place. Didn't they know the problems inherent in the engine? Allen and Patti had to confess they did not, but no one else did either when the model first came out.

Although their decision turned out badly, they could still say to each other and the world, "We aren't dummies! We didn't buy this car just because we thought it was pretty or because it was the only make that came in just the right shade of green. We had done our homework. We made a careful decision. The model was chosen 'Car of the Year,' so obviously other people, far more expert than we, also made an error in judgment."

This time, Allen and Patti's efforts did not pay off. Still, they knew they had tried, and knowing they gave the decision their best effort lent support to their sagging self-esteem and left no scar on their marriage. How would they have felt if they had made an irresponsible decision and picked the car for silly reasons? Surely, the incident would have taken a greater toll on their marriage.

SEPARATING DECISION MAKING FROM PROBLEM SOLVING

What I call decision making, some counselors call problem solving or conflict resolution. I prefer not to use those terms because words like *conflict* and *problem* imply that something must be wrong to warrant the need for a decision. This is an inappropriate connotation. There are circumstances that require couples to choose between pleasant alternatives — where to vacation, for instance. There is a decision to make when a couple is offered an investment opportunity, but there need not be any disagreement or conflict. Of course, many decision-making situations do involve a difference of opinion. But even these do not necessitate problems. Some people are capable of discussing their opinions without arguing, of exchanging ideas without becoming defensive. Only when people become defensive and cease to be receptive to other points of view, when their goal becomes winning the argument rather than exchanging ideas or making an effective decision, does the decision-making procedure become problematic.

This distinction is basic to the way I define decision making and problem solving. *Life is naturally full of decisions to be made — but people make problems.* If a couple is trying to decide what kind of car to buy, they are in a decision-making situation. If, in the process of deciding, they become upset with each other, then they have a problem. Problems are decision-making situations run amuck.

Sometimes you say you have a *problem* when you should more accurately say you have a *decision* to make. For example, you might conclude that a couple has a *problem* if the wife says to her husband, "Stanley, I feel frustrated when you clutter the house right after I've straightened up." You assume there is a problem because the house is cluttered, and that frustrates Stanley's wife. The couple does not have a problem to solve but a decision to make: what to do to alleviate the wife's frustration.

If the couple communicates to one another their thoughts and feelings on the subject, the resulting understanding may be enough to motivate Stanley to clutter less. If Stanley has reservations about trying to be neat, improved decision-making skills will help the couple arrive at a solution that is agreeable to both. If, however, Stanley responds to his wife's statement with, "Get off my back and quit nagging me!" *then* the couple has a *problem*. Stanley's hostile reaction has turned the situation into a problem.

Even the most serious problem is a decision that has gone off course. Take, for example, the case of a husband who discovers that his wife is having an affair. Most people would say the couple has a problem. Yet, even in this most serious circumstance, what they really have is a decision or series of decisions to make. They must answer these questions:

Will she end the affair?

Will he forgive her?

Do they still love each other?

Should he accept partial responsibility?

Are they going to seek a divorce immediately?

Are they going to seek professional counseling?

For most people, it would be extremely difficult to decide issues such as these without their emotions reaching the level at which decision making switches to problem solving. Yet, if the couple could manage to focus on the issues they must decide without becoming either hostile or withdrawn, they'd have a better chance of constructively working through difficult decisions without destroying their relationship.

I realize that the definitions for decision making and problem solving that I am proposing here are not the ones you would normally use in everyday conversation. You would typically say that if a husband like Stanley constantly clutters the house and his wife is annoyed by it, the couple has a problem. If your spouse had an affair, that would definitely be a problem in your book. Bear with me. I am not making this distinction between decisions and problems in order to argue that marital affairs are not problems. I grant that in general usage, an affair would be defined as a problem. What I ask is that, for a while at least, you suspend your usual definitions and adopt mine so that an important point about human interaction can be understood.

That point is this: If you want to, you can view even the most difficult and upsetting situation as a decision to be made and not a problem to be solved. You make it a problem if you allow yourself to become angry and vengeful or sullen and withdrawn. It doesn't have to be that way. If you want to, you can handle any situation without hostility. I'm not saying it is easy; I'm saying it can be done. Here, as in other areas, *attitude* is the key. Changing your usual definitions of decision making and problem solving can help you keep in mind the idea that a situation becomes a problem (as I have defined *problem*) when you let it. Neither the subject under discussion nor the content of a situation determines a problem. Emotions are not inherent in a given set of circumstances. This is evidenced by the fact that what is upsetting to one person is not necessarily so to another.

The skills that can help you keep your decision-making activities from becoming problem areas will be covered in the next chapter. At this point, let's look more closely at decision making.

THE SIX STEPS OF DECISION MAKING

The decision-making process itself consists of six logical steps.* Social scientists have found that most people naturally employ these steps to some degree when faced with a decision. Nevertheless, it is useful to state explicitly what many couples do implicitly. How much emphasis you give to each step and how much skipping back and forth you do are an individual matter. Most couples use the six steps as a guide to working out their own decision-making process, one with which they can feel comfortable.

The six steps are:

1. Identifying an issue about which a decision needs to be made
2. Identifying alternative courses of action
3. Evaluating the alternatives
4. Making a decision by selecting one of the alternatives
5. Implementing the decision
6. Evaluating the decision

1) Identifying the Issue

The task of identifying the issue can range from simple to difficult. Usually a couple can quickly agree that an area needs their attention. If the roof of their house begins to leak, a couple would not require much time to agree that a decision has to be made concerning the roof. If their son's

---

*There is some disagreement about the number of steps. Some scholars list as many as ten. Still, there is considerable consensus concerning the general sequence of events that constitute decision making.

91

teacher calls to advise them that Junior is a disciplinary problem, most couples would have little trouble agreeing that some decisions are in order. Sometimes, however, only one spouse will feel that an issue needs attention. The other spouse either does not see that anything is out of kilter or refuses to acknowledge it. When this happens, the identifying stage of decision making cannot be passed through so quickly. In the case of Junior, for example, if one parent feels (after talking to the teacher) that Junior is behaving as any normal, healthy boy his age should, the couple may not agree that a decision is necessary. When identifying the issue is difficult, a thorough round of communication will usually convince the skeptical spouse that an issue does exist — at least in the mind of his/her partner. Most people will eventually agree that something needs attention if they see that their spouse has strong feelings about it. Sometimes, however, one spouse will absolutely refuse to acknowledge that a decision needs to be made. When this happens, the other spouse must either drop the subject or treat the decision as an individual matter and devise a plan of action alone.

Some phrases characteristic of this first stage of decision making are:

> Let's make a decision about . . .
>
> Something's got to be done about . . .
>
> I guess the problem is . . .
>
> What can we do about . . . ?

Before moving on to Step 2, it is often wise to make sure you and your spouse are both talking about the same issue. Couples can get well into listing their alternatives before they realize they are working at cross-purposes. To return to our "boy in trouble at school" again, Mom may be thinking of ways to improve his behavior, while Dad is thinking of ways to get the child transferred to another class. A brief, summary type of statement by one parent or the other would help ensure a consensus concerning the issue being discussed. For example:

WIFE: Then we must decide what we can do to help Junior behave more appropriately.
HUSBAND: Yes.

Some couples communicate effectively in nonverbal ways. For them, too much verbal verification is unnatural. Try to avoid assuming too much, but don't stultify your exchanges with phrases that are uncomfortable either.

2) Identifying Alternative Courses of Action

This state of decision making is characterized by statements such as:

What do you want to do?

Maybe we could try . . .

I think we have two choices.

How about . . . ?

Fred was in this same situation and he . . .

Sometimes it is helpful to write down the alternatives as they occur to you. Making a list is useful when you want to consider a large number of alternatives, or when you are brainstorming and you want to keep track of the ideas you have already proposed. Lists are also appropriate when the issue being decided is not too personal or emotional. You might list resorts if you are trying to decide where to vacation. You might list apartment complexes if you are deciding where to rent an apartment. Mom and Dad might even make a list of all the ways they could encourage Junior to behave at school; however, it would certainly seem inappropriate to list on paper the alternatives open to you if you discover your spouse is having an affair!

Try not to pass judgment on each alternative as it is proposed. When ideas are immediately labeled "good" or "bad," two things are likely to happen: Either so much time is taken evaluating the first few ideas that you forget the other ideas you were going to suggest, or time runs out before either of you has a chance to bring out additional and possibly better alternatives. Also, immediate negative evaluation creates an atmosphere of censorship; if the first idea you suggest is labeled "wrong" or "stupid" immediately, you may hesitate to suggest another.

3) Evaluating the Alternatives

When a reasonable number of alternatives has been suggested, it is time to discuss the advantages and disadvantages of each. Try to avoid labeling the alternatives "right" or "wrong." These tags are too simplistic. Most likely each alternative has both positive and negative aspects. In most situations, finding a totally "right" alternative is probably impossible. What you are looking for is the *most* advantageous alternative. To discover it, you should consider the pros and cons of each possibility. Some phrases you might hear during this state of decision making are:

> This house has more square footage, but the other one has a larger backyard.

> If we go there for our vacation, we could visit Grandma on the way.

> Of course, we *can* invite the Browns to the party, but it will ruin the evening for me.

> I think that would be hard to do in the limited time we have.

The Evanses bought that model and they like it very much.

4) Selecting One of the Alternatives: Making a Decision

It is now time to decide which alternative to implement. Statements characteristic of this stage are:

> I like the first idea you had. I could live with that.
>
> Okay, what do you think we should do?
>
> I think we should divide our time between these two activities.
>
> Let's go ahead with . . .

When couples arrive at this stage, there is likely to be some disagreement. If, after considerable discussion, they are still unable to agree on a plan of action, several options are open to them:

a) One spouse can decide that the cost of further discussion is too high and simply give in. While he/she has not chosen the alternative the spouse favors, he/she will no longer oppose it.

b) The couple can realize that, in this case, neither one is going to get exactly what he/she wants and then agree that a compromise is in order. Each spouse will have to give a little to get a little.

c) The couple can agree to alternate the power of final say: This time, the husband decides; next time, the wife. This practice is useful for specific choices, such as what to do on Friday night. It can become extremely unwieldy when more nebulous categories are involved. I know of one couple who decided to alternate their "big" decisions. He would make *this* "big" decision; she'd make the *next* one. From then on, they argued interminably over the definition of "big." The problem: She complained that her decisions were not as "big" as his.

Still, you could alternate, for example, the responsibility of deciding

> what kind of car to buy,
>
> whom to invite to parties, or
>
> how to invest your yearly bonus check.

In any case, if you and your spouse should decide to alternate final say, incorporate into the decision an agreement that, once a final decision is made, it is to be *supported by both spouses*. No hindsight judgments should be passed, no "I told you so's" uttered. If you agree to this kind of arrangement, you should agree to support each other's decisions.

d) If you cannot reach a compromise and you don't wish to alternate final say, you can take your decision to a mediator — a marriage counselor, your minister, rabbi, priest, or anyone trained in mediating disputes. As you discuss the issue another time, a professional third party may be able to help you understand each other better and the whole situation may take on a new perspective. The mediator may be able to generate new alternatives, one of which might be acceptable to both of you. I have seen couples on a "one-shot basis," solely for the purpose of mediating a specific disagreement.

e) If the mediator is unable to help you arrive at a solution you can both live with, and if neither one of you is willing to change your mind, even though the situation is such that you must arrive at a decision, then one fairly drastic possibility remains: You can take the decision to an arbitrator — a person to whom you both agree to give final say. You and your spouse present your ideas and opinions to the arbitrator, and he or she makes the decision. For this method to work, you must both be prepared to abide by *and support* the arbitrator's decision.

5) Implementing the Decision

Once a decision has been made, the process is still not complete until the decision is implemented. So that both spouses understand what their responsibilities are, it is sometimes appropriate to assign tasks. Statements that might be made during this phase of decision making are:

Okay, that's the plan. Now how are we going to do it?

I think I'll need some help doing . . .

Why don't you get the addresses of our congressman and senators, and I'll write the letter.

6) Evaluating the Decision

After even the most careful consideration, you and your spouse may choose from your list of alternatives a plan that you later find cannot be implemented successfully. That is why it is sometimes wise to arrange a time for evaluating how well your decision is working out. Be prepared to admit it if your decision is a failure. At that point, you might want to return to Step 4 and choose another alternative.

MAKING GOOD DECISIONS

If we were always completely rational and well organized, we would probably move through these six steps in a totally systematic manner. But, people being the way they are, most couples find that they skip around, ignore some steps completely, and often deal with several at the same time. Couples also develop nonverbal signals that make it unnecessary to cover each step explicitly. As I mentioned earlier in this chapter, these steps are presented as a suggestion, not an unalterable format. Some decisions require more attention than others and should probably be handled in a more systematic manner. Others can quite successfully be arrived at by quickly exchanging a few nonverbal signals.

Give the ideas in this section careful consideration. Implement the ones that will improve the effectiveness of your decision making, but always be yourself. Don't try so hard to organize the decision-making process that you and your spouse feel uncomfortable.

Quality and Satisfaction in Decision Making

Sometimes the most important aspect of the decision-making procedure is whether or not the people who made the decision feel good about it. When a couple is trying to decide what movie to see, where to have dinner, or what color to paint the living room, it is more important that they both feel satisfied with the decision than that the decision be, by some objective standard, correct. In situations like these, there is probably no way to know what the best choice is anyway. Any evaluation of how "good" the decision is must center on how happy the deciders are with it.

In some situations, however, a decision can be evaluated as right or wrong, good or bad, productive or unproductive. Financial matters often provoke such situations. I see young couples, for example, whose undisciplined spending has landed them in financial hot water. At the time the couple charged their new stereo, new sofa, and new clothes, they were both very satisfied with their decisions. Nevertheless, the decisions were unwise, considering the debt the couple got themselves into. Financial investments must be made wisely. The ramifications of such decisions are far more important than the couple's feelings of satisfaction.

My wife and I once bought a rather large Samoyed puppy. It was love at first sight for the three of us. As it turned out, neither by wife nor I had anticipated just how large a Samoyed grows to be. I suppose we should have guessed from the fact that, as a puppy, his paw measured a good four inches across, but his soulful brown eyes had totally distracted us. Even as a baby, he knocked our smallest child down flat with his enthusiastic romping. As he quickly grew, he became more than a match for our oldest child as well. Unsure of just how large a mature Samoyed might be, we went to a kennel where adult males were boarded. To our amazement we saw white furry beasts that seemed almost as large as Shetland ponies. Sadly, we found a new home for our bounding bundle of white fur.

When you go to the pet store and survey the charming puppies, all the alternatives may be pleasing — but not all are sensible. My wife and I were both very satisfied with our choice, but we should have spent more time investigating the relevant facts. Had we done so, our decision might have been wise as well as satisfying.

Obviously, satisfaction and wisdom must intertwine. It would be foolish to assume that in every decision-making situation only one aspect or another is important. Still, it is fair to say that in any given situation, one of these aspects will need more attention.

Improving Satisfaction

Here are two helpful hints for increasing your satisfaction with the decisions you make:

PARTICIPATE FULLY IN MAKING A DECISION THAT AFFECTS YOU.

Consider this example:

> Harry and Mabel have decided to redecorate their living room. Mabel has always been in charge of decorating, but this time Harry is toying with the idea of painting the room a darker color for a more dramatic effect. Before he has a chance to discuss the idea with Mabel, however, she drops by the paint store and picks out two sample paint chips. Both samples are shades of off-white — one a yellowish tone, the other a grayish tone.

> Returning home, Mabel shows Harry the two samples and asks him which color he would prefer in the living room. Rather than mention his thinking on the matter, Harry decides not to make waves and resignedly settles for the yellowish chip.

Harry was not totally excluded from the decision-making procedure. He was asked to choose between the chips Mabel had picked out. Still, Harry does not feel satisfied with the decision. If the couple had discussed the issue more fully, Harry would have had an opportunity to suggest a darker color. Mabel might have liked the idea, or she might have explained that a darker color would make the room look smaller — a point Harry might not have considered. In any case, if Harry and Mabel had exchanged ideas and opinions, they both would have emerged from the discussion feeling that they had had their say in a decision that affects them equally. Participation does not guarantee satisfaction, but it does increase the chance that both spouses will feel good about the decision.

Married couples can encourage and help one another to participate more fully in decision making by asking each other for ideas and suggestions. Pay close attention to what your spouse is saying. Don't make light of each other's thoughts. If you don't understand something, check it out. Never ridicule a seriously proposed alternative. Some people don't express themselves as well as others. Give your spouse a chance.

AIM FOR A HIGH DEGREE OF CONSENSUS.

If you and your spouse agree that the alternative you've decided upon is the best one, then the decision is highly consensual. If one spouse is coerced by the other into accepting a decision, then the decision has a low level of consensus.

Let us say that Larry wants the children to be in bed promptly at eight o'clock every night. His wife Carol does not see the value in keeping to a schedule. She prefers to let each evening run its own course, depending on the needs of the children. Larry is upset by Carol's relaxed attitude. Carol is upset by Larry's obsession with eight o'clock. Realizing that a decision has to be made concerning the children's bedtime, Larry and Carol initially identify two alternatives: Carol can continue to put the children to bed when she feels they are ready (Carol's proposal), or Carol can stop playing with the children in time to have them in bed by eight o'clock sharp (Larry's proposal).

A highly consensual agreement:

As Larry and Carol communicated about this issue, Larry came to understand that Carol's main interest was for the children to have a prolonged period of positive interaction with at least one parent every day. (Between supper and bedtime was the most convenient time for Carol to devote to the children.) Larry, therefore, offers to spend time with the children every evening. Between both parents, the children's needs can be met in time for them to be in bed by eight o'clock. This accomplishes what Carol wants (sufficient attention for the children) *and* what Larry wants (eight o'clock bedtime). They both agree that this new alternative is best.

A less consensual agreement:

Both Larry and Carol want their own way, but they realize a decision must be made. Larry suggests the children be in bed sometime between eight o'clock and eight-thirty. He would prefer it to be eight o'clock sharp, and Carol would prefer no time limit at all. Nevertheless, in order to arrive at some kind of agreement, they decide to implement this new proposal.

Neither party is completely satisfied, but both feel it is a workable solution.

A low consensual agreement:

Carol says, "Do you want me to continue to get the kids ready for bed, or do you want to do it by yourself?" Larry says, "I wouldn't want that responsibility every night after a full day at the office." Carol continues, "Then quit complaining, okay?" "Oh, all right," grumbles Larry.

It is not always possible for couples — even those who enjoy a strong, loving relationship — to reach highly consensual agreements. Sometimes the cost, in terms of time and energy, is too great. It may happen that one spouse has very strong feelings about an issue, while the other feels that the effort necessary to reach a consensus is unwarranted. In such a case, the couple might be better off with one spouse accommodating the other, or even giving in completely.

If you feel the decision needs the support that consensus

generates, be prepared to invest the necessary time and energy to work out a highly consensual agreement. Try to think of new alternatives that will satisfy the needs of both of you. Be willing to reevaluate alternatives as communication with your spouse brings new information, perspectives, or values to light. Be honest about what you want, but avoid defensive reactions and stubbornness.

Remember that the more consensual your agreement, the more satisfaction you'll both derive from your decisions. This will provide you with a powerful incentive to expend the time and energy necessary to achieve that desired consensus.

Improving Quality

The quality, or wisdom, of a decision can also be enhanced. Here are several helpful hints:

GATHER AS MUCH PERTINENT INFORMATION
AS POSSIBLE.

Consider this example:

Ted just changed jobs and relocated his family. His previous position gave him the use of a company car, but his new position does not. Now they are a one-car family and will have to stay that way until they can afford another car. Ted's wife, Shelley, is upset. She feels trapped and frustrated because she can't get out when she wants to.

Before beginning to work out a remedy for the situation, Ted and Shelley should find out whether:

public transportation is available.

anyone at Ted's new office lives near him and would be interested in carpooling.

anyone in the neighborhood works near Ted and would be interested in carpooling.

GENERATE AN OPTIMUM NUMBER OF ALTERNATIVES.

Most people don't identify enough alternatives to make the best possible decision. Too often, couples devise just one course of action, and only if that fails do they think of alternative possibilities. This can be a frustrating experience. Negative feelings build quickly. In contrast, generating several alternatives at the outset can help a couple to arrive at the best decision more quickly. So work hard and put the best alternative on the ballot!

Of course, this procedure reaches a point of diminishing returns. Five or six alternatives are as many as most people can keep in their minds at one time. A couple could probably list fifty places where they'd like to vacation, but they couldn't effectively consider them all.

A list of possible alternatives for Ted and Shelley's predicament might look like this:

> Shelley could take Ted to work and pick him up on days she needed the car.

> Ted could carpool.

> Shelley could run all her errands in the evening and arrange rides for the kids' after-school activities.

> When Shelley needed the car, she could drive Ted to the bus stop (which is too far for him to walk), then pick him up in the evening.

FORMULATE A SPECIFIC PLAN.

If Ted and Shelley were to discuss their alternatives, but

fail to produce a concrete plan for sharing the car, then their decision-making efforts would be futile. A concrete plan of action is essential. There are, of course, times when a decision can be left hanging for a while, but not when both or one of the parties will continue to suffer frustration — as Shelley would, were she left without a car.

To improve the quality of your decisions, follow these three steps:

Gather as much pertinent information as possible.

Generate an optimum number of alternatives.

Formulate a specific plan.

CHAPTER 9

Problem Solving

When we put ourselves in the other person's place, we're less likely to want to put him in his place.

— *Farmer's Digest*

When ingredients such as sarcasm, name-calling, or sulking are added to the decision-making process, decision making becomes problem solving. Now the couple involved must struggle not only to make a decision, but to deal as well with each other's negative feelings and hostile actions.

I am continually amazed at the things over which people will argue: where to put the couch, what color petunias to plant, who made a wrong move playing cards with friends. Even when there are important decisions to make, such as whether or not one spouse should go back to school, some couples are still unable to concentrate on the issue at hand. Their discussions rapidly deteriorate into arguments. Their focus swiftly shifts from making a satisfying quality decision to winning an argument and defending egos.

These conflicts are not necessary. It is possible for people to make decisions concerning even the most sensitive issues without becoming upset with each other. *People can discuss without arguing. They can decide without fighting.* It is not always easy, but it can be done. The following recommendations can help you do it:

1) SEPARATE ISSUE FROM PERSONALITY

Discussions often dissolve into arguments when the focus switches from the issue at hand to the personalities of the debaters. If a couple is trying to decide whether or not to buy a sailboat, they are focused on the *issue* as long as they are discussing matters such as how much can they afford, how much weight their car can tow, how close is the nearest body of water for sailing. They can disagree as long as they are disagreeing about sailboats. But if sentences such as, "That's a dumb thing to say" or, "You're so lazy you won't even drive a few extra miles to have a whole day of fun" enter the discussion, the focus has shifted to the personalities involved. Not only do these verbal attacks diminish the chances of reaching a satisfying, quality decision, they also threaten the couple's overall relationship.

Why, then, do people tend to focus on personality rather than the issue at hand? For two major reasons: to boost their egos and show their power, and to "win" what they see as an argument.

Let's consider the first reason: ego. Calling a spouse "stupid" makes one feel smart. Bullying a spouse into compliance or silence makes one feel powerful. Spouses will often assume a condescending attitude toward each other, playing the role of a superior tolerating an inferior:

"Really, dear, your suggestion is quite ridiculous. How can you be so uninformed?"

Some people are more crudely aggressive in their style of attack:

"That's the stupidest thing I've heard. How could you be so dumb?"

Have you ever spent an evening with a couple during which one spouse constantly scolded and disparaged the other? It is a most uncomfortable experience. Once, in a restaurant, I observed a man exhibiting the ultimate in this type of behavior. His wife could not make a move without drawing criticism from him. As they attempted to decide what to order, he scoffed at every one of her suggestions. As they discussed their children and then the repair work apparently being done on their home, he continually tagged her ideas as "stupid." I was amazed at the length of time the wife continued trying to make pleasant conversation. Finally, I saw a slight glaze come over her eyes. It told me that her battered self-esteem had finally forced her to retreat. She no longer heard her husband's boorish harassment. What a miserable way for people to relate!

How do *you* respond to your spouse's ideas and suggestions? Do you call names and ridicule opinions? Do you, perhaps, feel a little more confident and a bit more powerful when you bring your spouse down a few pegs? *Listen to yourself*. Consider your motives. Are you building yourself up at your spouse's expense? If you have an uneasy feeling that you might be somewhat like the man in the restaurant, begin now to separate issue from personality. Address your comments to the issue at hand.

> Say: I don't think that plan will work because . . .
> Not: That's the stupidest idea you've had yet!

> Say: I don't feel you give my ideas any real consideration.
> Not: You're so bossy and pushy. I can never get a word in edgewise.

Now let's examine the second reason why people focus on personality: a desire to win the argument.

Some people see every decision, no matter how insignificant, as a win-or-lose situation. If the alternative they initially favor is the one decided upon, they win. If it is modified or discarded, they lose. For these people, focusing on personality rather than issues is just one more trick to make sure they come out on top. Such people are not interested in learning or expanding their understanding. They are not really interested in arriving at the best decision. Their major concern is winning what they see as an argument. They hate to be proved wrong. If they feel that their spouse has a piece of information that will threaten their position, they simply switch from issue to personality. One woman I know slips the word "fatso" into the conversation whenever she feels she is losing ground. Then, no matter how cogent the husband's reasoning was before, he completely loses his train of thought.

Listen to yourself the next time you and your spouse are making a decision. Are your comments helpful to the discussion? Or are they swipes at your spouse? Are you teachable? Can you stand the idea of learning something from your spouse? Can you admit error? Or do you attack your spouse with name-calling or sarcasm when you feel his/her ideas are too logical and you might not prevail? What is your goal when you and your spouse try to decide something together? Is it to share ideas, exchange information, and arrive at the best decision possible? Or, is it to make sure that your initial position is the one finally adopted, regardless of its merit or inferiority to your spouse's ideas?

Think about it. Listen to yourself. If you find that you're more pleased when you confuse your spouse than when you enlighten him/her, you have a problem. A decision-making session with your husband or wife is not the time to display verbal acrobatics. You are not dueling with your spouse. You are working together—not against each other. A good decision is in the best interests of both of you. Be teachable. Approach decision-making situations with a willingness to change your mind if your spouse has information you were unaware of before. Don't employ tricks such as calling your spouse "fatso" to derail his/her train of thought. You don't lose if your ideas are not adopted; you lose if you and your spouse make a poor or unsatisfying decision. Avoid bringing personality into the decision-making arena. Focus on the issue.

THE MARRIAGE SECRET

An Exception

There are times, however, when issue and personality cannot be separated: when the topic being discussed *is* somebody's personality (or at least some aspect of it).

When you and your spouse are trying to decide what car to buy, there is no reason for remarks about either of your personalities to enter the exchange. They would only cause problems. If, on the other hand, the issue you want to talk over with your spouse is something he or she does that bothers you, then naturally personality has to be discussed.

Decision-making sessions centered on these personal issues can benefit a marriage if they are handled with sensitivity. Too many people never tell their spouses when a habit is annoying to them. They make disparaging remarks under their breath or go around acting disgusted, but they never say, "Let's talk about it." People can continue to be irritated by their spouse's table manners, grooming habits, or nervous gestures for years and never directly confront the spouse with their irritation. Many people feel that such irritations are too petty to bring up. Still, they usually demonstrate their annoyance in some way, even though they don't intend to. It doesn't take too many little irritations to create an uncomfortable atmosphere. And, if the little irritations continue over a number of years, at some point the dam breaks and the pent-up feelings rush forth. It is not fair to unleash such a torrent on an unsuspecting person who was never told that a habit of his was annoying someone.

If a character trait or habit of your spouse bothers you regularly, you and your spouse need to decide what to do about it. It's not going to go away on its own. Of course, in discussions of this nature, feelings are sometimes hurt, pride bruised, and anger aroused. It can be difficult to keep this kind of decision-making session from becoming a problem. There are several ways to approach the situation, however, that steer you away from trouble.

Be sensitive to the idea that the irritating habit does not encompass your spouse's total personality. Try to separate this one bothersome trait from the individual as a whole. Be as specific as possible. When your spouse's rudeness bothers you, to say, "You're a terrible person" is not as accurate as, "You are so rude," which is not as accurate as, "You are rude to people who chatter about things that don't interest you."

A client of mine accused his wife of being a slob. Further communication revealed, however, that he really meant that his wife usually left the bathroom counter strewn with her toiletries. Deciding what to do about a messy bathroom is a much easier task than deciding what to do about a person who is a total slob. Being specific about what is bothering you is a less threatening and more useful approach to dealing with your spouse's upsetting habits.

Another way to make a discussion of personality traits less threatening is to use "I," as opposed to "YOU," statements. "YOU" statements are accusatory in tone. "I" statements are not as likely to provoke a defensive reaction. For example, people respond differently to, "You are so messy" than they do to, "I don't like a messy bathroom." One is an attack. The other is a declaration of preference.

Of course, being specific and using "I" statements will not completely eliminate the possibility that feelings will be hurt or tempers will flare. Trying to decide what to do when some aspect of your spouse's personality bothers you is always a delicate situation. But these precautions will help to prevent your decisions from becoming problems—especially if used in an atmosphere of kindness and concern for the welfare of the relationship.

2) ACKNOWLEDGE AND APPRECIATE THE SUBJECTIVE ASPECTS OF RIGHT AND WRONG

When two people marry, a certain amount of disagreement is inevitable. After all, they have been raised in different families. The variations in their backgrounds, no matter how slight, will give rise to differences in the way they see the world. All of us have definite ideas about what is and what ought to be. These ideas, however, are not necessarily grounded in fact. They are a product of the world view we have developed by virtue of our upbringing, the socialization process we have experienced.

When you and your spouse disagree, these concepts often come into play. It is helpful during disagreements to have an appreciation of the subjective aspects of right and wrong; to acknowledge that whether or not your spouse's opinion is correct in the absolute sense or not, your spouse believes that it is. Thus, his or her opinion is at least subjectively correct.

Sensitivity to the subjective correctiveness of your spouse's point of view can help you keep your decision-making efforts from becoming problems. Married couples are rarely in the position of choosing between options that are objectively right or wrong. There is no *right* name for a baby. There is only what each parent believes to be the right name. There is no objective way to determine absolutely what is the *right* movie to see or the *right* Christmas present for Uncle Harry. Usually the alternatives facing married couples are "OK," "good," and "better." The decisions to be made are not as black and white as whether or not to murder Uncle Harry in order to inherit his millions.

Still, some people insist on treating every decision as

having one right and one wrong option. This is *the right* area rug for the den; that is *the wrong* area rug. This is *the right* washing machine to buy; that is *the wrong* washing machine to buy. Such a rigid attitude precludes a fruitful exchange of ideas.

Consideration for the subjective aspects of right and wrong helps to create an atmosphere of respect, which is crucial to the healthy exchange of ideas. Most people become more close-minded and stubborn when their ideas are attacked as objectively incorrect. If, instead, each spouse considers the other's idea subjectively correct, you have two people who, while both believe they have a point, are trying to understand each other and reach a mutually viable solution. In this kind of atmosphere, communication and decision making can take place.

Another benefit that follows from an understanding of the subjective aspects of right and wrong is that it enables you to agree to disagree when the situation permits. Many subjects that husbands and wives argue about with venom do not necessarily require resolution. For example, if you and your spouse enjoy debating politics as an intellectual exercise, then, by all means, enjoy! Practically every political, social, economic, or artistic issue you might care to argue about can be debated effectively. If, however, you continually end up upset with each other over the same issue, then it may be time to resign yourselves to the fact that you cannot agree on that issue. Both of you have facts, figures, and expert opinion to support your view, yet neither one of you can convert the other to his way of thinking. It is not as simple as one plus one equals two, for neither opinion can be proven *objectively* correct. It is time to acknowledge that both of you are subjectively right and that you will respect each other's opinion, but that, because it is difficult for you to discuss this topic pleasantly, you will no longer debate it. You will agree to disagree and not bring up the subject again.

3) AVOID IRRATIONAL STATEMENTS

If you want to start a fight or keep one going, irrational statements are just what you need.

> You *never* have this house clean when I come home!
>
> You *always* embarrass me in front of my friends!
>
> You are the *dumbest* person in the whole world!
>
> I've told you a *million* times, I don't like to be tickled!

These are irrational statements. I calculated how long it would take to say, "I don't like to be tickled" a million times, and I am certain no one has spent 5,760 minutes repeating that phrase. I also know for a fact that the dumbest person in the whole world is Erasmus D. Gluckenheimer, an old high-school buddy of mine. As for *always* embarrassing you, well, that is rational only if your spouse has never—not even once—met or been around a friend of yours without embarrassing you. The same goes for saying the house is *never* clean. Can you really say it is always a mess? Hasn't it been clean even once—maybe for a party?

Of course, there are certain situations in which adverbs such as "always" and "never," exaggerations such as a "thousand times," or superlatives like "laziest," may be accurate. You could say you always burn your mouth when you swallow hot chocolate over 170 degrees F., or that you have *never* been to the moon. A prison guard might accurately say to a lifer. "I have told you a thousand times not to talk while standing in line!" And if you knew Erasmus D. Gluckenheimer, you could say, in all honesty, that you know the dumbest person in the world!

However, in most situations, "always," "never," exaggerations, and superlatives lead you to irrational statements. And irrational statements do not contribute to rational discussion or effective decision making.

Let's look at a hypothetical couple struggling to implement a decision they have made, and see how irrational statements can cause problems.

Ruth had been feeling increasingly depressed. She felt unattractive and unloved, and her eroded self-image was beginning to affect the way she interacted with her husband, Robert. Finally, Robert and Ruth sat down to discuss her growing depression and to decide what to do about it.

Communication revealed that Ruth was used to more verbal affection than she was getting in her marriage. So Robert and Ruth decided that Robert would try to verbalize his love and affection more frequently. While Robert explained that he found this difficult to do, he was willing to try. Four months later, however, Ruth was not feeling better.

ROBERT: *(exasperated)* Ruth, what do you want me to do?
RUTH: It wouldn't make any difference if I told you. You don't do the things I ask, anyway.
ROBERT: What do you mean?
RUTH: I mean, I've asked you a thousand times to say "I love you" every once in a while, but you never do it. You're the most insensitive man I've ever met!

Obviously, Robert and Ruth must communicate better about Ruth's feelings and evaluate the results of the decision they made four months earlier. Ruth's irrational statements,

117

however, only interfere with their attempt to give the subject the serious attention it needs.

Some people pick up on their spouse's irrational statements to the exclusion of the real issue. For example, Robert might say, "You haven't told me anything a thousand times, Ruth. Don't exaggerate. And it's not true that I never say, 'I love you.' I said it last Christmas, on your birthday, and on our anniversary. And you and I both know Fred Faux Pas is the most insensitive man in the world. You've said so yourself a number of times."

In this manner, Robert uses Ruth's irrational statements as a diversion; he does not focus on her hurt feelings or his inability to verbalize emotions.

Robert and Ruth could go on for some time bickering over just how many times in their relationship Robert has said, "I love you." He might challenge her to prove she's asked him a thousand times to be more verbal. Of course, if he can remind her of just one instance when he did say, "I love you," he can dismiss her plea for him to be more verbal. After all, she said he *never* says, "I love you." Now she must admit that on at least one occasion he did. Ruth was wrong—case dismissed!

If Robert is not the kind of person who picks up on irrational statements as a diversionary tactic, he may be the kind who becomes very discouraged by them. One sad and frustrating fact I have learned over the years is that people are often unaware of how hard their spouse is trying. He or she may not be succeeding; nevertheless, when a person is trying hard, he finds it extremely painful when his efforts go unrecognized. A Sunday-school teacher I had as a child was fond of saying, "Discouragement is the devil's most powerful ally." There's a lot of truth to that statement, for when people become discouraged they stop trying.

Let's assume that Robert has been trying hard to say "I love you" aloud. It is very difficult for him, as it is for many men and some women I have counseled. Nevertheless, he has succeeded a few times. He managed it on Christmas, his wife's birthday, and on their anniversary—all within three and a half months of each other. That's practically once a month! Robert thinks he's doing pretty well. He's trying to do even better, but at least he's come this far.

Ruth, on the other hand, is frustrated. She has told Robert how she feels. They've had a big discussion about it. They made a decision; yet, as far as she is concerned, the results have been negligible. So, when Ruth says she's told Robert a thousand times what she wants but he never does it, Robert is discouraged. He tried. He had some success, but Ruth did not recognize it. Robert feels that Ruth has no appreciation for what he has accomplished, so why should he continue to try?

People who do not make a practice of using their spouse's irrational statements as diversionary tactics and aren't discouraged by the comments, may simply be hurt, for these statements are often heavy-handed, overpowering, or just plain mean.

Sentences such as "I've told you a thousand times what I want but you never do it" and "You're the most insensitive person in the world" have the potential to inflict deep pain. There are so many more constructive ways to get one's point across. Yet, I am continually amazed at what people who claim affection for one another will say to each other. For example:

> "I've shown you a hundred times how to
> change a washer, but you always louse it up.
> You're the most uncoordinated person in the
> world."

> "You never take time to spruce up anymore.
> You're the sloppiest person around. I've asked
> you a thousand times not to wear those crud-
> dy old shoes, but here you are wearing them
> again."

I cannot think of any justification for speaking to another person this way. Of course, using words like "always" and "never," phrases such as "a thousand times," superlatives like "sloppiest," are habitual for many people. Irrational statements are firmly entrenched in colloquial American speech patterns. You may not even notice that you're using these irrational phrases; you may be unaware of how much you're hurting your spouse. By making a conscious effort to eliminate irrational statements from your conversation, however, you show that you are not guilty of cruel, hurtful attacks on the person you say you cherish.

One more type of irrational statement warrants con-sideration: *irrational generalizations.* This type takes the form of inflating a deficiency in one area of competence into a deficiency in a much larger area. Let us say, for example, that your spouse has a difficult time remembering to record checks in the checkbook. He or she does not spend money wildly, however, is a careful comparison shopper, able to dicker effectively on major purchases like cars, and has made several small but wise investments. One night, as you are balancing the checkbook, you see that entries have again been omitted from the register. Frustrated, you confront your spouse:

> "I get really upset when you're so careless with money!"

Careless with money? A person who is a careful shopper, a wise investor, and a shrewd bargainer is not careless with money. Don't generalize from *forgets to enter checks* to *care-*

less with money. Address your remarks to the matter in question:

"I get really upset when you forget to enter checks in the register."

A decision needs to be made concerning the check register. Focusing on that specific matter will help you make that decision. Generalizing to other areas might cause your spouse to feel frustrated and unappreciated. The decision then moves closer to becoming a problem.

4) AVOID ASYNDETIC CONVERSATION

Asyndetic (tenuously connected) conversation is sometimes referred to as "hitchhiking" because, in this form of conversing, one person "picks up" on a certain aspect of what another has said and moves the conversation to what he/she is reminded of. Then someone else "picks up" on a new line of thought and focuses briefly on it. The words "That reminds me" are often heard during asyndetic conversation.

In social settings, asyndetic conversation is a common way of exchanging information. Have you ever started a conversation on one subject and suddenly found yourself discussing a totally unrelated topic? "How in the world did we get onto this?" you ask. The answer is, you "hitchhiked"— as Mary and Frieda did in the following exchange:

MARY: Lousy weather we're having. I don't think I've ever seen so much rain.

FRIEDA: And it's not only been wet for days, it's been cold too.

MARY: Really miserable. My coat got so soaked yesterday it was still wet this morning.

FRIEDA: A friend of mine, who spent two years studying in England, told me all his friends had two raincoats, so one could dry out while they wore the other.

THE MARRIAGE SECRET

MARY: Who do you know who studied in England?

FRIEDA: Howard Breakard.

MARY: Don't know him. Did he come back with a British accent?
I just love the way they talk. A holdover from my Beatle-
crazed adolescence, I guess.

FRIEDA: I love British accents too. I watched a whole show on PBS
about Australian aborigines just to listen to the narrator's
accent.

MARY: You watched a whole show just to hear the narrator's accent?
Did you hear what he was saying as well? One of the most
interesting classes I ever had in college was an anthropology
course on primitive cultures of the world. Did you know that
Australian aborigines are the only known group of primitive
people to practice male contraception?

There you have it. From rain to sex in five minutes.
Nothing unusual or harmful about it. Actually, rather en-
joyable, for as you hit the highlights of each other's experiences and share a few opinions you get to know one
another in a broad, general way.

But asyndetic conversation is fine only for casual exchanges. When you and your spouse are trying to make a
decision, you must stick to a topic until it is covered to both
parties' satisfaction. You cannot hitchhike from idea to idea,
never finalizing anything.

Because so many of our casual conversations progress
in an asyndetic manner, it is hard to break the habit for the
purpose of serious discussion. Consider the following example:

Nancy says, "John, when I hear you talk to the children
in such a cold, angry way, I feel frightened inside. I think
I'd rather hear you yell at them the way other fathers yell."

JOHN:

Relevant	*Asyndetic*
I'm sorry, Nancy. I didn't realize I was	Well, I don't think it's a good idea to yell at

scaring you. What I meant to do was keep from flying off the handle. I guess I tried so hard my words came out cold, and I can see how that might be scary. Still, I don't think yelling at the kids would be a good idea. My dad yelled all the time and I hated it. Let's think of some other alternative.

the kids. My dad used to yell, and I hated it. He'd scream at us in front of our friends, and some of them wouldn't come back to play at our house. I want our home to be a place where my children's friends feel welcome. It would mean a lot to them, I'm sure, if their house were sort of a neighborhood gathering place.

Nancy's senses have reported something that frightened her. She has something she wants to talk about. She shares her feelings with John. When John answers in a relevant way, he responds directly to her feelings. He sticks to the subject Nancy brought up. When John responds asyndetically, he picks up on one aspect of Nancy's statement (yelling at the children) and goes off on a tangent (making the house a neighborhood gathering place). He does not address himself to Nancy's feelings at all. If we followed the conversation further, it might very well travel off track even more.

Of course, there is nothing wrong with John explaining to Nancy how he feels about the way his father used to yell; that information will help Nancy understand his behavior. Still, his explanation should be part of a relevant reply to Nancy's statement and not a way of hitchhiking to another topic altogether.

In this example of asyndetic conversation, the "guilty

party" was not trying to avoid discussing his spouse's thoughts and feelings. Rather, he simply commented on the first thing that came to his mind without considering how pertinent his response was to his wife's statement. Sometimes, however, when feelings are running hot, people use asyndetic conversation to avoid talking about subjects that threaten them.

"Well," responds an angry wife, "my house may not be the cleanest, but it's better than that pigsty your sister keeps !"

"If you think I'm hard to please," retorts an injured husband, "just look at how fussy *you* are!"

These sentences begin exchanges that will probably wind up far afield from the original topic.

When your spouse approaches you with something that needs to be discussed in depth, don't change the subject. Make your comments relevant to the particular issue. Be aware that it doesn't take much to throw a conversation off the track.

Not only is asyndetic conversation detrimental when you and your spouse are trying to make a decision, but it should also be avoided when you are sharing your primary feelings, checking out a sensory perception, or anytime you have serious matters to discuss. In those instances it will only detract from your ability to communicate.

Save asyndetic conversation for everyday chitchat, where it will not pose any problems.

5) USE META-COMMUNICATION WHEN NECESSARY

Meta-communication is a fancy term that simply means *the process of communicating about communication*. When you and your spouse step outside your conversation and talk, not about the subject you have been discussing, but about the *way* you have been discussing it, that is meta-communication.

If you are yelling at, or withdrawing from, each other, nothing constructive will be accomplished. If emotions are getting out of hand, things may be said and done that can damage your relationship. At such a time, while it might be appropriate to postpone the conversation to a later date, it might also be appropriate to meta-communicate—talk for a few minutes about what is going on between you.

People complain that if they have to keep stopping their discussion to talk about talking, they'll never get anything done. They have a point. Meta-communication, like role reversal, is somewhat clumsy. It does not slip easily into a conversation. It requires a definite break in the exchange. Certainly, it would be difficult to use the technique frequently. Couples who try it, however, report that frequent use of meta-communication is not necessary for the technique to have the desired effect. After using it a number of times, many people develop a single phrase or nonverbal cue to remind their spouse of something they discussed during previous meta-communication sessions.

A couple who recently came to me for counseling derived great permanent benefit from using meta-communication only a few times.

David and Colleen's courtship had been brief. They had not discussed controversial subjects before marriage. Their relationship was based on fun and games. Both, however, were intelligent, educated people. They understood that their decision to marry had been made in a romantic haze. Now they were eager to know, in an intellectual way, the person they loved physically and emotionally. But, as marriage made necessary the discussion of a wider variety of topics, they began to realize that, unfortunately, their opinions and ideas were often in opposition.

Worse yet, they seemed unable to talk through their differences. Whenever they began to disagree, Colleen became tongue-tied. She often cried. The couple usually ended up not talking at all.

They came to counseling, hoping a professional third party could help them constructively work through their areas of disagreement. Nevertheless, instead of wading through their problems, I began by having them analyze what went on between them when they tried to communicate or make decisions.

David and Colleen were impatient at being asked to take this indirect approach. They did not believe their problems were caused by a lack of communication skills. Still, we began by concentrating on the dynamics of their communication.

What emerged from David and Colleen's meta-communication was interesting. Apparently, David was in the habit of pressing his lips into a hard, thin line whenever he and Colleen disagreed. David did not execute this mannerism with the intention of upsetting his wife; nevertheless, it had a powerful effect on her. Colleen had been raised to value the open exchange of ideas. Now she felt completely censored. Whenever they disagreed about anything of substance, David's posture became rigid, his facial expression disdainful. "His lips go into a thin line," Colleen explained, "and I can't discuss anything in that kind of atmosphere."

Besides feeling censored, Colleen admitted she was concerned about what kind of a marriage she'd gotten herself into. Open intellectual exchange was important to her; now she found herself unable to discuss ideas with the man she had married. As a result, she wound up in tears, fearful and confused. Things were not turning out as she had expected.

For his part, David had been unaware of the messages his posture and expression were sending to Colleen. He knew he had angry feelings when Colleen disagreed with him, but he thought he had been controlling them. Now he realized that his voice, his expression, his tense body had been like neon signs. The question now was, "Why ?" Why did David behave thus when Colleen disagreed with him?

Further discussion revealed that David felt intimidated by his wife's academic record and intellectual background. David was the first member of his family to go to college. In Colleen's family, everyone was college-educated. David was continually improving his scholastic skills, but his grades were not yet as high as Colleen's. David believed in equality of the sexes, but his history was dominated by a highly authoritarian father and an ethic that encouraged male domination. Quite simply, David felt threatened by Colleen. If they disagreed and she proved to have more information or superior logic, his insecurity was heightened. The tense body, the disdainful look, and the hard, thin, lip line were all defensive maneuvers engineered by his naturally vigilant ego defense system.

David and Colleen realized that their difficulties were not as directly tied to the topics they discussed as to what passed between them during their discussions. Typically, both David and Colleen enjoyed a healthy intellectual encounter. They could handle the idea that another person might have a point more valid than theirs. In their marriage relationship, however, other factors were at work. When David and Colleen had trouble communicating, they needed to stop discussing *what* they were discussing and communicate about the *how* and *why* of their interaction.

David and Colleen found that after they had successfully

meta-communicated a few times, they did have to repeat the entire process if David began to fall into old patterns. By touching her finger to her lips, Colleen could re-communicate all they had previously discussed. That simple gesture on her part said:

> You are doing it again. But I love and respect you. There is no need to feel threatened. We are two people exchanging ideas and information. No one is up. No one is down. Yes, we are trying to convert each other to our own point of view, but our worth as people does not depend on "winning" this debate. Our worth lies in being the kind of people who want to learn from each other.

If you feel you need to talk about what is going on between you and your spouse when you try to communicate or make a decision, ask yourself the following questions:

1. *Does my spouse have mannerisms that annoy me?*

If they interfere with your communication, they need to to be discussed. I remember one man who felt hurt and insulted by the way his wife flipped her wrist as if to dismiss his ideas as ridiculous. After years of irritation, he finally checked out the meaning of the gesture. To his astonishment, his wife was unaware of the movement. It was a mannerism acquired from her mother, that held no particular meaning for her.

2. *What are your goals in communication?*

Are your decision-making sessions actually disguised power struggles ? When you are ostensibly deciding what sofa to buy, are you really deciding who makes the decisions in your marriage ? Is your goal a show of power rather than an effective decision?

3. *Do you need to vent your feelings?*

Decision making can cause emotions to run high. You might want to talk about these emotions if you feel they are preventing you from focusing on the issue at hand. Of course, you have the option of postponing further discussion until you have your emotions under control. But it might be even more useful to talk about the emotions. Try to get to your primary feelings. Are you hurt, frightened, or frustrated by your spouse ? Are you reacting to your spouse's opinions or the way in which he or she presents them ? Are you surprised to find you and your spouse involved in this kind of argument ? Do you feel distant from this person whom you thought you knew well ?

We often assume that when our spouses become impatient, they are impatient with us for not following the logic of their argument. In fact, they may be upset with themselves for not being able to explain their position more persuasively. In this case, hurt feelings on our part are unwarranted.

Are you sometimes afraid there might be a flaw in your argument and that you will have to admit to an error in judgment? Does that thought upset you? Will your worry spark an irrational drive in you to establish and maintain some kind of superior position?

Find out what is going on in your conversations!

DECISION MAKING VERSUS PROBLEM SOLVING: A RECAP

The process of making decisions together offers married couples an opportunity to learn more about each other's opinions and feelings, an opportunity for each spouse to see and enjoy how the other's mind works. Decision making can be a source of experience, information, and even pleasure if it is approached in the right spirit.

Of course, you may disagree with your spouse's ideas. You may become frustrated because your spouse does not see what is obvious to you. Still, if you focus rationally on the subject at hand, you'll find you can cope with legitimate disagreements (see Chapter 8). If you do find, however, that your decision-making efforts usually turn into arguments, then try to implement the suggestions made in this section on problem solving:

Separate issues from personality.

Acknowledge and appreciate the subjective aspects of right and wrong.

Avoid irrational statements.

Avoid asyndetic conversations.

Use meta-communication when necessary.

CHAPTER 10

On the Bright Side

Cheerfulness, like spring, opens all the blossoms of the inward man.

— Jean Paul Richter

Human beings are capable of a wide range of bright and beautiful emotions. Our lives have moments of sweetness because we can experience feelings of love, joy, and pride. When we share these things with another person, a special kind of bond is formed. Those moments of sharing contribute depth and strength to the marriage relationship.

So far, we have dealt almost exclusively with negative emotions. This is because they are the ones that cause trouble and need more immediate attention. However, in counseling, I find that if couples spend their sessions concentrating solely on their problems, they bog down in a quagmire of negativism. To prevent this, I periodically help couples focus on what is positive between them.

While you have been and will continue to be upset at times by what you learn about your spouse, it is also probable that many of the things you have learned or will learn are positive—happy surprises. It's important for you to deal properly with your good feelings as well as your bad. When something your spouse does makes you feel happy, try expressing that happiness.

"When I see you laughing and playing with the kids, I feel happy all over."

When you feel appreciation, don't always let yourself off with a perfunctory "Thank you." Occasionally, you should spell it out:

"When I'm really rushed and you take the time to help me with my work, I really appreciate it."

For some people, it is easy to express feelings such as love and appreciation. For others, it makes them very uncomfortable. I have found that people who have difficulty expressing positive feelings usually substitute what they think for what they feel. When their spouse performs in a local theatrical production, they say, "Your performance was really a standout," but not, "I was so proud of you." They say, "This was one marvelous evening" instead of, "I feel so happy when I do things with you." Often this substitution is unconscious. Rarely do they have anything against saying, "I love you," "I'm proud of you," "I feel happy around you." It's just not the way they talk. "Gushy-mushy" stuff embarrasses them.

It's not that complimenting a performance or saying an evening was terrific is bad. They are nice things to do. And there is nothing wrong with expressing feelings indirectly—with praise, gifts, or hard work—on behalf of a loved one. These all carry positive messages. But every once in a while people need more than praise, gifts, hard work, or whatever nonemotional currency their spouse offers them. They want a flat out "I love you!"; a straightforward, "I am proud of you"; an uncamouflaged, "I feel happy with you."

When the happy surprises pop up, don't let the opportunity pass to express your positive feelings. Don't miss the moment. An associate of mine once told me how just such a moment became the turning point in her marriage.

She had been married for five years. It hadn't been a bad marriage, but it hadn't been all she'd hoped for either. At the end of their fifth year, her husband was offered the chance to invest in a business deal that promised to turn a sizable profit. The operation was not illegal, but it was dishonest. Without hesitating, he turned the offer down.

The woman was deeply impressed by her husband's decision. She had never given much thought to this aspect of his character. She knew he was basically a law-abiding citizen, but she had never considered the degree of his honesty. The moment could have passed unheralded if she had something like, "I think that was the right thing to do." Instead, she looked straight at her husband and said, "That was the right thing to do, and I am so very proud of you for being an honest man." For an instant, they communicated; they touched in a way that people do only if they share their feelings.

That moment marked the beginning of new growth in their stagnant relationship. She realized that there were still many things to learn about the man she had married. He felt a renewed sense of worth in his wife's eyes.

Does the thought of expressing something openly, such as "I am so very proud of you," make you edgy? Think about the things you say to special people on special occasions. It is a good indication of how able you are to say what you feel. If you realize that you rarely express in words what you are feeling, then begin to think about doing so! When your spouse does something that impresses you, speak out.

> "You handled that embarrassing situation
> with grace. I was so glad you were there."
> "I didn't know you could fix a radio. You're
> so good at so many things."

If you recognize an admirable quality in your spouse, comment on it.

> "You have stayed so cheerful and positive
> through this difficult time. I have really ap-
> preciated your support."
> "You are such a forgiving person. I don't think
> I could have taken what you've taken and
> still be civil to those people."

A friend of mine realized after several years of marriage that his wife was an extremely patient person. He'd never really thought about it until a series of events led him to see it was one of the things he loved most about her. He wanted to say something, but couldn't seem to get it out. He never has told her how he felt. He loves her and she knows it. She loves him too. They have a good marriage. Still, this man missed an opportunity to deepen his marital relationship.

There will be times in the future when you will be pleasantly surprised by your spouse; times when you will realize he or she has talents or abilities you weren't fully aware of; times when you will feel strong, positive emotions well up within you. Plan now to share these. Your spouse may be a little flustered at first if he or she is not accustomed to it, but don't let that fluster *you*. Practice makes perfect. If you can force yourself to express something that feels awkward at first, a few experiences may make the words flow more naturally. Take it slow. Don't force yourself to the point that you turn off to the idea completely. Try to find out from your spouse how important it is to him/her that you verbalize your feelings. Some people can never hear "I love you" often enough. For others, constant repetition makes the phrase stale, a mere gesture. Some people prefer fewer words and more hugs and kisses.

Different people have different needs. Yet, despite these variations, I firmly believe that no relationship can reach its full potential if the partners never directly express their positive feelings for each other.

CHAPTER 11

Why Bother?

True marriage
Is not my devotion
To you,
Nor is it
Yours to me.
True marriage
Is our devotion
To us.

— Lois Wyse

THE MARRIAGE SECRET

You have just read almost one hundred and fifty pages telling you how to build a succcessful marriage in an unpredictable world. Some of the things probably sounded easier to put into practice than others, but they all take time and effort. There is no getting around it—building a good marriage takes work! But, as with most valuable things, that effort makes it more valuable still.

Nevertheless, working toward a successful marriage may sound very complicated and laborious. It is legitimate to wonder why people bother to marry at all.

Historically, people have done so because the family unit served many practical purposes. Faced with an agrarian lifestyle, men and women married to produce offspring who would provide the helping hands needed to secure food, shelter, and protection.

Throughout history, marriage has also joined kingdoms and estates, averted wars, and sealed political treaties. In all of this, the feelings of the individuals involved were not central to the union or its preservation. Marriage was considered much too important an institution to be influenced by the ravings of the heart.

In America today, however, most people do not marry in order to survive, add power and prestige to their family names, or seal business agreements. There is little in our American culture or economy that *requires* us to marry. Every year more social and legal supports of matrimony are struck down. Yet every year more people get married. It's true that divorce is increasing as well, but the majority of divorced persons remarry. The total number of marriages every year exceeds the total number of divorces. Eventually, most Americans marry. What are modern Americans seeking in this most ancient of human rituals? What is it, then, that people feel they can achieve only by tying a legal knot?

I believe the answer is as uncomplicated as the question is complex. The answer is commitment. When people marry, they intertwine themselves legally, they join their families, and they announce to everyone who knows them that they have committed themselves to making a life together. This makes marriage serious business, because if it doesn't work out, the partners must go through the legal hassle of a divorce; they must shoulder responsibility for what their families suffer; and they must deal with the embarrassment of having failed.

Through cohabitation, people can find love, companionship, sex, and shared financial responsibility. Of course, there is emotional upheaval when live-in lovers part, but the ramifications do not compare with those of divorce. Marriage is the real thing—the ultimate commitment. In marriage, people hope to establish a relationship that will develop a history and have a future. Many people still dream of growing old and wise surrounded by loving children and grandchildren. An impossible dream, some say. But for those who want to reach for it, the commitment of legal marriage is the place to start.

The ideas and techniques presented in this volume are not aimed solely at helping you establish a relationship for the here and now. Rather, this book has been written to guide those of you who want your marriages to last a lifetime. As I've said before, marriage is a lifetime of getting to know each other. In a lifetime, people change, situations shift, and relationships take on new dimensions. If you hold on to rigid expectations and refuse to flex, you'll have difficulty finding happiness. If you allow yourself to wallow in disappointment at a bad turn of fate, you'll never understand the power inherent in your privilege to determine your own attitude.

THE MARRIAGE SECRET

Understanding the "marriage secret" and learning the skills presented here will help you preserve your marriage in this unpredictable world. If lifelong marriage is what you want,

> Accept the idea that there were things you did not know about your spouse when you married.
>
> Be prepared for changes in your spouse.
>
> Be prepared for the intrusion of unforeseen events into your marriage.
>
> Understand the value of flexibility.
>
> Believe in the power of your attitude.
>
> Express your primary feelings.
>
> Control your anger.
>
> Do your best to make wise and/or satisfying decisions, but always acknowledge the ever present element of chance that will influence their outcome.
>
> Try to prevent decisions from becoming problems.
>
> Verbally express your positive feelings.

Then, after years of changing and learning, of growing together, you and your spouse may say to each other those memorable opening lines of Robert Browning's "Rabbi Ben Ezra":

> *Grow old along with me!*
> *The best is yet to be,*
> *The last of life, for which the first was made.*